CHAPELTON

THE MAKING OF A TOWN

Paul Roberts & Isabelle Taylor

Turnberry Consulting Ltd
41-43 Maddox Street, London, W1S 2PD, UK

Designed by Common Curiosity
Printed by Blackmore Ltd

Every effort has been made to contact and
acknowledge the copyright holders, but if any have
been inadvertently overlooked the authors will be
pleased to make the necessary arrangements at the
first opportunity.

ISBN 978-0-9569078-5-1

'TOWN PLANNING IS NOT MERELY PLACE PLANNING, NOR EVEN WORK PLANNING. IF IT IS TO BE SUCCESSFUL IT MUST BE FOLK-PLANNING.'

Patrick Geddes, 1915

CONTENTS

FOREWORD
10 YEARS OF PROGRESS

The publishing of this book marks 10 years since we set out on a trajectory to build Chapelton, a new, standalone town at Elsick, land that has been a family home and estate for six centuries. Admittedly, at the beginning of the process, we never imagined embarking on anything of such a scale, but the venture quickly grew. It soon became clear that there was an opportunity to strike against the pattern of development of recent years – houses tacked onto houses with no long-term thinking – that has, to our mind, done much to diminish the built quality of Aberdeenshire, as well as the country at large, and undermine the great traditions of Scottish urbanism. We wanted to create a positive legacy for urban development in the North East.

To ensure that Chapelton became something altogether different, altogether better than modern precedents, we deliberately went down two unconventional routes. The first was, in 2008, to set up the Elsick Development Company to promote the scheme, by which means we could retain control of the project and thus the ability to safeguard the original intent. The second was to follow in the footsteps of the Earl of Moray at Tornagrain and engage Miami-based DPZ, led by Andrés Duany, as master planners. Duany is a pioneer of New Urbanism, a design movement that counters suburban sprawl by advocating walkable neighbourhoods with a range of housing types, shops and jobs, that lessen car dependency and promote community. The practice has won international plaudits for its sensitive and context-driven approach to urban planning, and it was important to us that Chapelton would be grounded in the best traditions of local town planning, vernacular architecture and materials.

The diggers started on site in 2013. At the time of writing, Chapelton has 260 residents, a teashop, nursery, hair and beauty salon, parks and allotments. There is still a long way to go. Possibly 40 years will pass until the town reaches its anticipated size, by which point we will have up to 8,000 homes, schools, health and retail facilities, a series of green spaces and more.

This publication is intended to be a record of progress so far, and a statement of intent for what we hope we will achieve. It is, perhaps, premature for a book about Chapelton to be written now. Yet already we can see the objectives we had for the town coming to fruition. The most significant of these is the social dimension. There is a noticeable community feeling at Chapelton, and this spirit is gathering momentum as the development progresses. We are all learning lessons as we go, but it can probably be safely said that when you arrive at Chapelton, you know you are somewhere out of the ordinary.

Reaching this point has been hugely challenging. We were probably unprepared for just how complex the planning and development process can be. But throughout, we think we can be proud that we have held onto our original intent – to create a place that will endure, in the best tradition of Scottish town building. Achieving this vision would not be possible were it not for the dedicated team behind the project – urban designers, architects, landscape designers, planning consultants, engineers, solicitors, planning authorities, building contractors – and thus our closing thought is one of thanks to all those involved. ◆

The Duke and Duchess of Fife,
April 2018

INTRODUCTION
BUILDING A LEGACY

How many towns in Great Britain come to mind that have been created within the past four decades, completely new settlements that have sprung from virgin soil? Probably very few. That is because such endeavours involve such heights of complexity – financial, regulatory, logistical – that proposals for them rarely leave the drawing board. Yet, this is the task that is being undertaken on 840 hectares of farmland, eight kilometres south of Aberdeen.

In October 2013, ground was broken at Chapelton, a new town of up to 8,000 homes. It has the potential to become the largest town in Aberdeenshire. The driving force behind its inception and ongoing development is The Duke and Duchess of Fife. The majority of Chapelton sits on the Elsick estate, land that has been in their family continuously since the fourteenth century, except, that is, for an interlude following the 1745 Jacobite rebellion, when they found themselves on the losing side. For generations, the gently rolling acreage, largely hidden from view by low rounded ridges, has been farmland, albeit indifferent-quality farmland. In 2007, however, the integrity of the estate came seemingly under threat. A long-awaited bypass around Aberdeen had been announced on the west side of the property. Furthermore, the local council was intent on substantially increasing the supply of new dwellings in the county, and the estate, located hard by the A90, sat squarely within one of its identified corridors of development. There was, the Duke felt, a real risk that Elsick or its near surroundings would end up engulfed with housing. Rather than leave it to an unknown fate, in 2008 the Duke and Duchess – who were then Earl and Countess of Southesk, not acceding to the dukedom until 2015 – formed the Elsick Development Company (EDC) to promote the building of a new, standalone town on the site. At this point, they had little clear vision of the physical form they wanted Chapelton to take, but they did know that they wanted it to be different, and better, than what was being built elsewhere.

The previous decades had seen Aberdeenshire fall prey to a nationwide contagion – sprawling, low-quality residential developments that are stitched, little by little, onto existing settlements. Across the UK, vast tracts have been given over to suburban estates and retail parks, largely devoid of character. It is a land-hungry, short-termist approach to growth. Moreover, it is antagonistic to community creation or aesthetic experience, both of which are ingrained human aspirations.

Since the early days of settlement, mankind has evinced a cross-cultural preoccupation with building cities that respond to more than the functional requirements of a physical place for living.[01] Most of us instinctively feel the importance of our urban surroundings on our psyche and, in turn, our wellbeing. The link is not easy to explain but there is measurable evidence of the relationship between environment and happiness. Several scholars have documented that opportunities for social interaction within a neighbourhood positively correlate with the mental health of residents.[02] Meanwhile, a 2009 study found that a perception of beauty or aesthetic character plays a significant role in community satisfaction, substantially larger than any individual demographic characteristic.[03] This is supported by a 2011 investigation into 10 international metropolitan cities that concluded the more inhabitants felt that their city was beautiful and the more they felt connected to the people within it, the more likely they were to report greater levels of happiness.[04]

From its outset, Chapelton was envisaged as a place that would satisfy these deep-seated, inherent appetencies. It was to be an antidote to the prevailing pattern of single-use housing estates and a return to the best traditions of north-east Scotland's historic towns and villages: a community-centric place, both socially rich and aesthetically stimulating. Houses, healthcare, shops, schools and employment would sit shoulder to shoulder; residents' daily needs would be a short walk from their front door. Buildings and the public realm would be designed to a calibre and ambition that few modern developers contemplate, injecting beauty into everyday life.

A decade after the formation of the EDC, these objectives are being met. Chapelton welcomed its first inhabitants in 2015. It is a tangible, growing settlement with a budding community ethos. Residents gather to host Burns Night street parties and annual summer barbeques; study groups have come from as far as Japan to learn from its best practice urbanism. It is still at an early stage in its existence; there is perhaps another four decades of growth ahead of it. The journey here has been complex and, on occasions, bumpy and there will, no doubt, be more hurdles to meet. Yet, Chapelton should already be recognised for striving to break the mould of twenty-first-century development.

The following pages outline the story of its achievement to date. They fall into three sections. The first is historical in nature; beginning in the twelfth century, it briefly describes Scotland's rich tradition of town building, which Chapelton is informed by in shape and spirit. The second section moves to the present day, and narrates the development of Chapelton from the genesis of the idea, through the planning process to its ongoing evolution. The final chapter is devoted to the town's design – its master plan, landscape and architecture. It culminates in a series of plans and photographs that visually documents the extent of the town's development to date and examines, from a physical perspective, what sets Chapelton apart.

For Chapelton certainly is a different beast from the vast majority of residential schemes being pursued in the British Isles today, both in its design and its social aspirations, not to mention its scale. What we hope to do in these pages is to sketch the profound challenges involved in creating new settlements of quality and community that can rival those of the past, but also to emphasise that these difficulties can be overcome. When this happens, as at Chapelton, the difference in the place thus created is clear. ◆

CHAPTER ONE
SCOTLAND: 900 YEARS OF NEW TOWNS

Over the past 900 years, the nation has given life to a succession of new towns and villages, which today constitute one of the central strands of Scottish identity. These new settlements were founded in bursts of activity, in the Middle Ages, the Age of Enlightenment and the post-war years, each leaving a dramatic and lasting impact upon the country's urbanism. Each era approached the task with their own objectives and aesthetic bent, yet they established a rich legacy of planted settlements in Scotland, of which Chapelton represents the inheritance.

MEDIEVAL BURGHS

In the early twelfth century, the landscape of Scotland was radically changed. From the 1120s, there began one of the most coordinated, sweeping episodes of town planning ever to take place in Britain. The credit for initiating this enterprise goes to David I (r. 1124-53) who, over his three-decade reign, was responsible for the creation of some 20 burghs, settlements possessing exclusive trading rights conferred by royal charter. David's immediate successors followed suit, so that by the end of the Canmore dynasty in 1286, places such as Edinburgh, Perth and Elgin had been chartered as royal burghs, whilst lay lords and religious magnates had also, with monarchical approval, established their own baronial and ecclesiastical burghs, including St Andrews and Kelso.

The creation of these new towns was a politic stratagem. David, having grown up in England where he married an Anglo-Saxon heiress, had first-hand experience of the Anglo-Norman court, its feudal system and its towns. His systematic foundation of new towns in Scotland was a means of economically strengthening the kingdom on the Anglo-Saxon model through the provision of carefully controlled centres of commerce. The burghs were granted a monopoly on the trade of goods from their rural hinterland; thus, produce from the sherrifdom of Perth, for instance, could only be sold within the limits of Perth on fixed market and fair days. Restrictions on foreign imports and exports were even more keenly safeguarded. By stimulating and concentrating trade within the new burghs, David laid the foundations for a more prosperous, modern Scotland – which, happily for the Crown, made for more efficient taxation and increased revenues – whilst also cementing royal authority.[01]

David's town-founding policy should be viewed as part of a growth in urbanisation that was then spreading across Western Europe, but it is all the more noteworthy because there is no documentary or archaeological trace of towns in Scotland prior to his reign. This absence of evidence for urban settlements has led to the conclusion that the royal burghs were Scotland's first urban settlements.

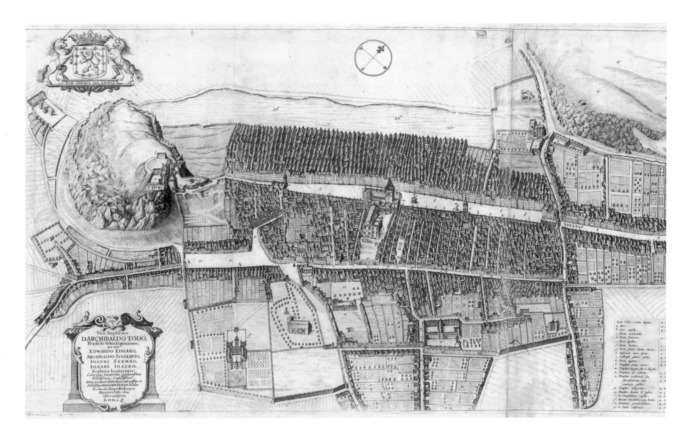

The reality, though, may be less black and white. The reigns of David's predecessors are known as the 'Dark Age' of documentation, and historians of recent decades have contended that we are not justified in assuming that no urban life existed hitherto on the sole basis that no written proof survives. Indeed, it has been argued that the very fact that the burghs flourished so readily suggests that the concept of nucleated settlements was not new, and examples of some significance existed prior to the 1120s that facilitated the adoption of David's burgh system.[02]

Any burghal predecessors that did exist, however, would almost certainly not have been deliberately planned. David's burghs, meanwhile, were strategically laid out to meet the socio-economic ambitions he had for them. With the conferring of burghal status came formalised planning of streets and plots. The layout of a typical burgh was a single main street lined with tofts, or burgage plots, of consistent length and width. This arrangement was not unique to Scotland; reflecting David's Anglo-Norman outlook, it was the traditional plan for medieval towns from the south of France to the north of England.[03] Physically manifesting the burghs' function as a commercial centre, the focal point of the town was a market place, frequently simply a bulge in the main thoroughfare. It was here that the civic buildings were sited: parish kirk, tollbooth (town hall), tron (weigh station) and a mercat cross (signifying the right to trade). Houses, though none survive from this period in Scottish towns, would have been built close to the road edge at the front of each toft. The tofts stretched in long, thin lines running at right angles from the main street and often demarcated at their rear by narrow back lanes parallel to the principle axis. As the burghs grew, these lanes sometimes became thoroughfares in their own right. For the most prosperous burghs, such as St Andrews, additional parallel streets were laid out in line with their success.[04]

Above /
John Geddy's plan of St
Andrew's, c.1580. Founded
as an ecclesiastical burgh,
parallel main streets were
arranged to converge on a
new cathedral.

From Elgin to Edinburgh, Forres to Dumfries, the early burghs are stamped by
a deliberate and standardised planning approach. Variations are in evidence,
prompted by the natural topography or existing castles for instance, but
overwhelmingly street layouts, plot alignments and land use possessed 'a
coherence consistent with a centralised perception of town development from the
outset'.[05] Planning was, it is thought, the responsibility of surveyors, sometimes
directly appointed by the king. Scant information is known about these men,
although Mainard the Fleming is recorded as having been invited to lay out St
Andrews following his experience of planning at Berwick, and similarly Ranulf
of Haddington was appointed at Glasgow, having previously successfully laid
out Haddington.[06] What is clear is that the surveyors went about their task with
methodical consideration. Ayr, for instance, was planned as a new town in the
early thirteenth century. The main street was plotted far enough from the river to
allow room for the tofts, between which vennels were staggered so as to prevent
traffic congestion.[07] Furthermore, archaeological research suggests that this formal
ordering of space was subsequently upheld by town officers through the enforcing
of building regulations.[08]

While little built fabric survives, the highly considered, formalised footprint
of these early burghs survives as a testimony to the systematised approach to
town planning that was introduced to Scotland by David I and his successors.
The formula thus created yielded places that, in many cases, have evolved into
substantial settlements, influencing generations of townscapes up to the
present day.

Below /
i) Edinburgh, 12/13th century
ii) Forres, 12th century
iii) Perth, 12/13th century
iv) St Andrews, 12th century

Key /
♟ Castle
✝ Church
✠ Market Cross

i)

ii)

iii)

iv)

If the first chapter of Scottish town building was launched by the Crown in the twelfth century, the second was marshalled this time by the combined forces of market capitalism and intellectual enlightenment in the eighteenth century. By the 1750s, Scotland had entered a period of political stability and financial growth after decades of turmoil. Following the parliamentary Union with England in 1707 until the final suppression of the Jacobite cause in 1746, the nation had been beset by invasions, uprisings and economic depression. Their cessation at the midpoint of the century opened the door to radical transformations within Scottish society. Old patterns of feudal hierarchy waned and individualistic capitalism waxed. Intellectual life flourished with the birth of the so-called Enlightenment, saving Scotland, as one commentator has encapsulated, 'from the relative cultural isolation in which she had passed the seventeenth century' and placing it at 'centre of the thinking world'.[09] Collectively, a spirit of progress fuelled an age of modernisation and improvement.[10]

This ideology had repercussions for the urban setting. With the Enlightenment doctrine that man, guided by reason, could effect positive change, came an aspiration to shape society for the better through its built environment. This set in motion an agenda for urban improvement based on amenity, visual aggrandisement and spatial order.[11] Across Europe, a preoccupation with the 'ideal city' was emerging, but the idea particularly took hold amongst the Scots. As the country hurtled towards industrialisation, demands grew from the landed elite and urban bourgeoisie for towns to be remodelled in ways that reflected the country's new prospects and remapped their social geographies.[12]

The most lucid and best-known example of this is the construction of Edinburgh New Town. Between the 1750s and 1830s, the royal burgh of Edinburgh breached its medieval crag-and-tail confines to expand onto empty fields north of the Old Town. Heralded as one of the world's finest examples of classical town design, the undertaking resulted in a panorama of squares, crescents, terraces and public buildings united by the neoclassical ideals of symmetry, stateliness and hierarchy that quickly became a blueprint for Scotland's urban improvers.

While the New Town can be read today as a rational Georgian set piece, the actual story of its realisation was more a matter of providence than calculated planning. Suggestions for an urban expansion to Edinburgh were first posited in the seventeenth century, but it was not until the 1750s that anything came of the idea. By this time, Edinburgh was acutely overcrowded. Buildings of 11 or 12 storeys were not unusual, with density reaching up to 1,750 people per hectare in the High Street. All sectors of society lived cheek by jowl in the closely packed tenements where sanitation was poor and fires were common.[13] 'In no city in the world,' wrote Daniel Defoe in the 1720s, do 'so many people live in so little room as at Edinburgh'.[14] Following the collapse in 1751 of a six-storey tenement in the High Street, in 1752 the

Convention of Royal Burghs published a pamphlet entitled *Proposals for carrying on certain public works in the city of Edinburgh*, which recommended 'enlarging, beautifying and improving the capital'. The *Proposals* was couched in a combination of fiscal and patriotic terms. 'The meanness of Edinburgh has been too long an obstruction to our improvement, and a reproach to Scotland', it stressed. Its 'present form and situation' had driven the nobility, and consequently their money, to London. Following the Union and its demotion as a seat of government, Edinburgh was rapidly sinking into insignificance. To rescue it from political and economic obsolescence, it was argued, the city needed to be remade, and in such a form that it would rival the 'healthful, unconfined situation' and 'beauty and convenience' of London.[15] Doing so would bring higher rents, public revenues and a general affluence that would permeate beyond Edinburgh to benefit the country as a whole.

The New Town was, therefore, conceived to be a 'Mayfair-on-Forth', as Charles McKean has styled it; an exclusive residential enclave distanced from the cramped insalubrity and social hotchpotch of the medieval nucleus, to attract 'people of fortune and a certain rank'. It was to have no commerce or, excepting churches, public buildings.[16] It was a political move, driven by the city officials.

In 1766, a competition was launched 'inviting Architects and others to give in Plans of a New Town marking out streets of a proper breadth, and by-lanes, and the best situation for a reservoir, and any other public buildings, which may be thought necessary' to be sited on Council-owned greenfield land across the Nor'Loch from the Old Town. Beyond an allusion to 'order and regularity', the brief was vague.[17] The winning proposal by James Craig took the form of a Union Jack, a political commentary on the role of Scotland within the Union, but the unwieldiness of the triangular blocks meant it was soon revised into a classic axial grid. The orthogonal plan consisted of three parallel streets – Queen, George and Prince's – stretching east to west with a large square at either end. Space was ordered with regulated hierarchy from the main boulevards and squares designed for Edinburgh's patricians, to the secondary, narrower lateral Rose and Thistle streets for tradesmen, and the mews lanes for stable hands, accessed through openings in the street blocks.[18] In October 1767, ground was broken on the first house.

Mayfair-on-Forth, though, never materialised as envisioned. From its earliest days, it became clear that the anticipated aristocrats would not be tempted back from London, and thus the concept was shifted towards a greater social mix, with a focus on the merchants and professionals that made up the emergent middle classes. Craig's intent for large terraced houses – inferred by the size of the building stances – modelled on those of London was intermixed with flatted tenements, albeit often disguised by palatial frontages. Furthermore, its persona as a purely residential suburb was soon jettisoned: the Theatre Royal was begun at the eastern end of Prince's Street in 1768, and the Physicians' Hall and Assembly Rooms were completed on George Street in 1775 and 1787 respectively, by which time shops had started to open on Prince's Street.[19]

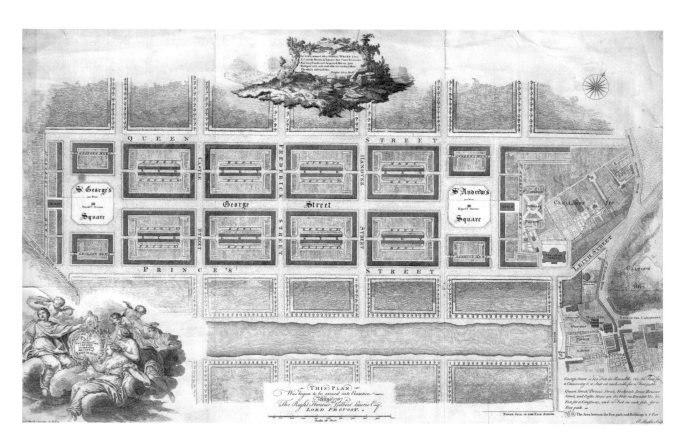

By 1820, most of the area covered by Craig's plan was built or under construction. Its success led to the development of a Second New Town to the north from the early 1800s. Although spoken of as a single concept, Edinburgh New Town is in fact a series of urban extensions built speculatively over the first quarter of the nineteenth century by individual landowners.[20] These later phases shared Craig's harmonious sequence of hierarchical streets, emphasised by the detailing of the architecture. Moreover, they were united by design controls imposed with increasing rigour by the Town Council.

The Council did not develop any of the land contained within Craig's plan itself. As was traditional in Scottish property tenure, plots were feued to individual builders. However, eager to achieve the ordered standardisation which rested at the heart of the 1752 Proposals, the city magistrates sought control of the urban aesthetic through the passing of a series of New Town Acts and development regulations. The first New Town Act, for example, issued in 1767, made general provisions to ensure such matters as consistent pavement widths and building lines. The initial limitations, though, proved insufficient to curb the individualistic inclinations of the house builders, and completed portions were criticised for their want of grandeur and poor proportions. Controls passed in the 1780s grew increasingly prescriptive and were strictly enforced.[21] Plans and elevations had to be approved by a committee; building heights were restricted; dormer windows were prohibited; and, perhaps most important of all for the future homogeneity of the New Town, there was an almost exclusive use of finely dressed squared ashlar.[22]

The Council's vision for a coherent, ordered townscape took a leap forward with its appointment of Robert Adam, the most celebrated architect of the day, to design Charlotte Square in 1791. Adam had a particular prowess for designing unified house frontages, and this skill was employed to full force in the square, where terraces of individual buildings were treated as a single palatial entity. Each side of the square, imposing yet elegant, was an exercise in harmonious town composition. It was to set an influential model for subsequent phases.

Compared to the maze-like Old Town, with its confined plots, narrow wynds and high-rise tenements, the New Town was an urban revolution. It encapsulated the classicising zeitgeist of geometry, rationality and hierarchy, creating a spatially ordered realm a world away from the medieval townscape on the other side of the Nor'Loch. Its spacious boulevards, dramatic vistas and neoclassical architecture advertised Edinburgh's undiminished status as a European capital and, moreover, established a civic code for urban improvement that was to spread across Scotland.

Edinburgh's modernisation initiated what can be perceived as a 'self-conscious competition' between the nation's towns.[23] Six years after Edinburgh's New Town was begun, Glasgow Town Council commissioned surveyor James Barry to draft plans for lately purchased lands beyond the congested medieval centre. The proposals were set aside until 1782, when Barry's 'Plan of the City of Glasgow,

Gorbells, Caltoun and Environs' was published and work began on laying out a parallel grid of streets interwoven into existing roads that had been built earlier in the eighteenth century. As at Edinburgh, the Council never intended to act as a developer itself; the enterprise was a speculative one intended to appeal to Glasgow's rising mercantile, manufacturing and professional population. In marked difference to Craig's self-contained design for Edinburgh, however, Barry's New Town was planned as an open-ended grid to enable boundless expansion. This was soon to happen. From 1800, the grid was extended to the adjacent Meadowflat lands and further west to the Blythswood estate.

Aberdeen's expansion in the early nineteenth century also took the form of an elongated rectangular grid. Aberdeen was then growing rapidly in inhabitants and affluence. Its medieval warren of narrow, winding streets and steep topography was no longer adequate to hold the burgeoning population, nor did this layout facilitate trade access into the city. In 1794, surveyor Charles Abercrombie was appointed to plan new routes into the burgh from the north and south. His proposals were bold and ambitious. They rested principally on the creation of a 'direct, straight street' running westwards from the mercat cross, opening access to greenfield land where 'a large addition to the town by a regular plan divided into building lotts' could be constructed. This was no easy feat; it necessitated the levelling of the summit of St Katharine's Hill and the bridging of the Denburn Valley.

Work began on the new thoroughfare, called Union Street, in 1801 and four years later, the 18-metre viaduct over the Denburn was completed. Large expanses of slum property were demolished in the process.[24] Union Street was designed to be a grand, residential road accessing a fashionable new suburb, but the westward migration of Aberdeen's well-to-do was less pronounced than had happened in Edinburgh New Town.[25] Uptake of building plots was sluggish and, thanks to the expense of the infrastructure works, the city was driven to bankruptcy in 1817. Nonetheless, as the new axis of city life, the construction of Union Street reshaped Aberdeen in urban and social terms, bringing it into line with the tide of improvement that was sweeping the whole country.

The Planned Village Movement

The enthusiasm for improvement in Scotland was not restricted to cities alone. In the second half of the eighteenth century arose a vogue for the creation of planned villages by landowners inspired by the Enlightenment zeitgeist. The planting of new rural settlements was not totally novel, but examples pre-dating this period are rare. Partly due to the trading monopolies held by the royal burghs, Scotland had little tradition of the nucleated village model – cottages, church, inn, manor house, smithy grouped around a green or street – that prospered in England. As late as the 1790s, over 60 per cent of the Scottish population lived in small, scattered communities – fermtouns, kirktouns or miltouns – or isolated dwellings, where farming was the only occupation.[26] This settlement pattern, though, was radically transformed by new economic conditions and the wide-ranging changes ushered in by the era of agricultural improvement.

The eighteenth century saw nothing short of a revolution in the economy of the Scottish landed estate. New concepts about crops, cultivation and livestock breeding were imported from England, and old fermtouns were wiped away in favour of standardised, individual farms, far bigger and more efficient than the former system. As a result, large numbers of people were dispossessed from their homes and livelihoods.[27] Conscious of the social upheavals caused by their improvements, eighteenth-century estate owners seized upon the concept of the planned village as an opportunity to absorb the displaced population and provide employment for former labourers. 'By tradition, no landowners were more deeply and sincerely paternalist than the Scots,' wrote Thomas Smout.[28] Towns, they believed, were dens of iniquity, whereas villages were the perfect environment to keep people virtuous and dutiful. Yet, the planned villages were more than philanthropic enterprises alone; the reasons behind the phenomenon were many and complex.

In the first instance was profit. Landowners wanted to maximise the income from their estates. By creating local centres of population, and thereby encouraging skilled workers to remain in the countryside rather than emigrate to towns or overseas, they would retain rental gains and, furthermore, have a guaranteed market for the produce grown on the new enclosed farms. Planned villages were a key cog in the economic revolution that spread across the whole country. Linked to the growth in the fishing and textile industries and improvements in communications, landowners invested to establish local industries and built

new harbours to provide diversification in an economy that had long been overly dependent on subsistence farming.[29]

The earliest planned villages date to the 1730s, with one of the first being Ormiston in East Lothian, founded by John Cockburn to replace an existing fermtoun. It was not until after the Jacobite cause collapsed in 1746, though, that village formation occurred with any regularity. By the time the trend began to wane in the 1830s, numerous examples had been either laid out afresh or took shape from old settlements remodelled beyond recognition. The precise number of planned villages created is debated – estimates range from 150 to 450 – but the greatest concentration lay in the north east of the country and on the southern margins of the Grampians.[30]

The nature of the places defies neat categorisation, but most can be classified by their employment base as either small-industry, fishing or factory villages. The former was the most plentiful. Ormiston, built for cloth workers, was the prototype. The boom in textile manufacturing led directly to the planting of settlements including Tomintoul, begun in 1779 to fulfil the Duke of Gordon's objective of launching a local weaving and linen industry, and New Keith, laid out from circa 1750 by the Earl of Findlater as a rival centre for the textile trade in Banffshire.[31]

When the economic mainstay of the whole settlement was a single factory, the settlement is designated a factory village. Here, the driving force tended not to be the landowner but entrepreneurial industrialists, such as David Dale. The latter was the founder of New Lanark, a model village in the Clyde gorge established upon the

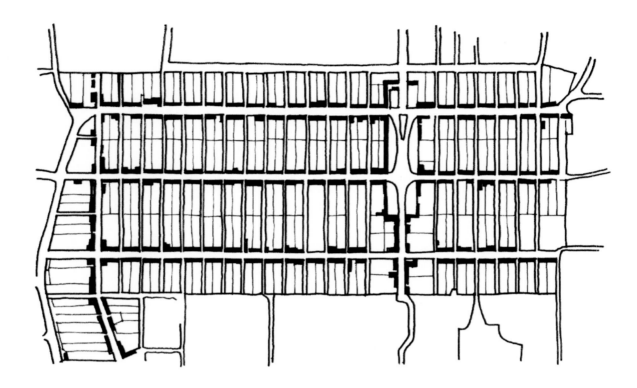

recommendation of Richard Arkwright, inventor of the water-powered spinning frame that transformed cotton production. Harnessing the energy of the Falls of Clyde, from 1785 Dale financed the building of water-powered mills and the erection of a whole village around them to house his workers.[32]

Whatever their categorisation, the most distinguishing point about the planned settlement is that they were conceived to a physical plan, with a prescribed street pattern and, frequently, architectural regulations. Inspired by the Enlightenment belief in the influential power of the environment, as well as the celebrated precedent of Edinburgh's New Town, the villages embodied the precepts of neoclassical urban design in miniature – axes, grids, squares, symmetry.

At their simplest, the villages took the form of linear, single-street plans, perhaps with a secondary cross street or square, as at Swinton in Berwickshire. Narrow parallel lanes gave householders access from the main street to the rear of their plots, and, particularly in the North East and Highlands, led to back lanes running the length of the property boundaries. So far, their designs seem to owe much to the precedents of the medieval burghs; but, where they differ is in their emphasis on neoclassical regularity and spatial order. This is evident in the layout of squares. The square was the focal point of village life, in particular in its role as the site of the markets. This importance could be reflected in their large size; that of Newcastleton in Roxburghshire, for example, spanned over two fifths of a hectare.[33]

More elaborate plans followed a grid-iron layout, possibly to increase density on small sites or to permit future expansion in later years.[34] New Keith was laid out

Above /
New Keith, laid out c.1750 by the 5th Earl of Findlater on a regimented grid-iron plan interrupted by a wide market square.

Above right /
Inveraray, begun c.1750 to an ambitious cruciform plan by the 3rd Duke of Argyll to replace an existing settlement that was demolished to make way for a grand new castle.

Below right /
Executed by John Adam and later by Robert Mylne, Inveraray's layout and architecture was amongst the most ambitious and elegant of the planned villages movement.

with four parallel streets and a large central square. Fochabers in Moray – which was built by the Duke of Gordon to replace an old burgh that was found to be inconveniently close to Gordon Castle – was composed of a main thoroughfare flanked by two parallel streets, in between which were service lanes accessing the rear of properties in an arrangement strongly reminiscent of Craig's grid for Edinburgh New Town. Designed circa 1776 by John Baxter, who had trained in Italy, Fochaber's layout was amongst the most ambitious of the village plans, informed by axiality and geometry.[35] In Aberdeen, meanwhile, the Town Council laid out Footdee, a model fishing village, from 1808-9, based on two regimented, open squares surrounded by uniform housing. Footdee – which was to prove an inspiration to Chapelton's designers nearly 200 years later – was planned by John Smith, who was to become one of Aberdeen's principal architects.

Not all landowners were interested in aesthetics, but a number employed prominent practitioners to design their villages. Thomas Telford, who was amongst the foremost engineers of his day, laid out Pulteneytown in the Highlands. James Gillespie Graham, whose Moray Estate in the Edinburgh New Town is regarded as one of the finest examples of Georgian urban planning, was engaged to set out Kyleakin on Skye and contributed to buildings in Inveraray.[36] Inveraray, built by the Duke of Argyll, was laid out by William and John Adam, father and brother of the more famous Robert, with individual buildings designed later by Robert Mylne, architect of London's Blackfriars Bridge.[37]

Few settlements were designed to make such an elegant statement as Inveraray, but all tended to share a common physical formula. Domestic stances were long and rectangular. Houses were laid out directly onto the pavement, in part to prevent inhabitants keeping unsightly dunghills in their front gardens, which were a common sight in fermtouns. As was typical of Scottish development practice, the landowners left house-building to the feuars.[38] Yet frequently they sought detailed control over the villages' architecture through the implementation of building regulations. The British Fisheries Society, a quasi-governmental organisation founded to establish planned fishing villages in the Highlands, drew up a series of 17 detailed regulations in 1788 that specified the materials, heights, building lines and so forth of settlers' houses in its villages. These were of such importance to the Society that at Ullapool (founded 1787) its agent was instructed to raze contravening dwellings that had sprung up there by the mid 1790s.[39] At Grantown-on-Spey, feuars undertook to build houses that were 'regular and fronting the street with stone and lime walls and cover the Roofs with Slate and build the Dykes round the Gardens with stone five quarters high'.[40] Other landowners were less strict. At Strichen in Aberdeenshire, for example, the sole stipulation was that houses should be built with two stone chimneys.[41]

By the 1840s, the enthusiasm for founding new settlements was in decline. The increasing centralisation and mechanisation of industry effectively put an end to the movement come the mid-point of the century.[42] That the industrial towns

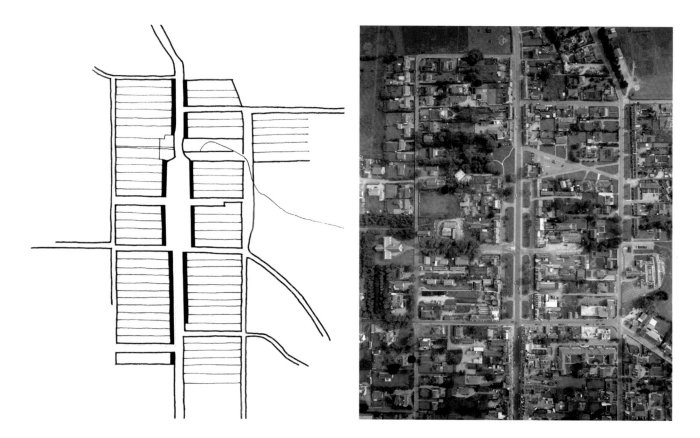

Grantown-on-Spey, founded 1766. The formal geometry of the Georgian grid plan established a legacy that continues to shape the town today.

expropriated the economic base of the villages has led many to dismiss the planned villages as failed experiments.[43] Yet, of the hundreds of new settlements that were created, only a very low proportion failed to survive.[44] Inveraray, for instance, never became the textile hub that the Duke of Argyll had envisioned, but it did develop into a successful service centre.[45]

The planned villages played a fundamental role in the economic revolution of eighteenth- and nineteenth-century Scotland. By providing an effective force in attracting incoming migration and stimulating new employment, they helped to address the dispossession caused by land reforms. Furthermore, as examples of comprehensive urban design informed by principles of the age of improvement, the movement is a singular achievement of regional planning at a scale not attempted since the creation of the royals burghs in the Middle Ages.[46]

UK NEW TOWNS

The next major episode in Scotland's history of town building arose out of the devastation wreaked by World War II. Unlike the planned villages, whose key driving force was private individuals or organisations, this chapter was state impelled. The war prompted resounding changes in attitudes towards governmental intervention in all spectrums of public life, not least town planning. The extensive bomb damage within UK cities and the subsequent housing shortages – half a million homes were destroyed and a further half a million were left marred – sent physical planning soaring up the political agenda. The newly created Ministry of Town and Country Planning commissioned Patrick Abercrombie, Britain's leading authority on urban planning, to produce a blueprint for the future of the London region.

His Greater London Plan, published in 1944, proposed the relocation of one million people into eight new satellite towns and other expanded towns in an orbit around the capital. This concept of decentralisation proved compelling. It was adopted as the basis of the landmark New Towns Act of 1946, intended to relieve the post-war housing demands not only for London but nationwide.

Fundamentally, the New Towns Act addressed the problems of bomb-riven, overpopulated inner cities through the government-controlled creation of new planned settlements in less crowded areas, countering the all-too prevalent trend for sprawling ribbon expansion. It was more than a programme for the built environment, however; it was conceived as a path towards the creation of a fairer society. The utopian communities were to embody the modern, democratic aspirations of a new Britain.

The Act gave rise to 32 New Towns in England, Scotland, Wales and Northern Ireland, built upon the precepts formulated by the Reith Committee in 1945-6. The Committee recommended that the towns should be designed for 30,000 to 60,000 residents, housed in low-density family housing using a 30-units-per-hectare maxim; provide a job for each inhabitant; and be organised as self-contained neighbourhoods, linked by open green spaces.[47] They were principally designated during three waves of activity: from 1946-50, with the objective of decentralising crowded cities; from 1961-4, to combat housing shortfalls; and the final generation in the late 1960s and early 1970s, chiefly aimed at encouraging regional economic growth. Each town was shaped by the substantial powers brought into force by the New Towns Act. Central government identified the sites to be developed and appointed a development corporation to direct the growth of each town, to which the Treasury allotted an annual budget. The Act entitled the corporations to compulsory purchase land at agricultural value, to draw up statutory master plans to control development and to grant planning permissions.

The first Scottish site to be designated was East Kilbride in South Lanarkshire in 1947. Intended to decentralise overcrowded Glasgow, which had some of the worst housing conditions in the UK, it was envisaged as a self-contained town of 45,000 residents surrounded by greenbelt.[48] Glenrothes, the second of Scotland's New Towns, was designated the following year to serve the growing coal mining industry in Fife. Both shared the same essential planning model as the other phase I new towns: a zonal plan comprising a town centre, low-density housing grouped in neighbourhood units and a separate industrial area. By the time the next town was designated – Cumbernauld in 1955 – the preoccupation with segregated uses and low densities was under fire by younger generations of designers. Cumbernauld, also built to relieve Glasgow's housing pressures, experimented with the most cutting-edge lines of thought within town planning. To foster greater urbanity, the master plan (submitted 1958) was inspired by compact Italian hill towns. Planner Hugh Wilson prescribed 65 homes per hectare and, unlike East Kilbride and Glenrothes, these were not structured into separate neighbourhoods.[49]

The modernist tour-de-force of Cumbernauld's design was the town centre (built 1963-7). The eight-storey megastructure built atop a hill brought Le Corbusier's Radiant City to North Lanarkshire. Architect Geoffrey Copcutt implanted civic, commercial, residential and parking facilities within a single, multi-deck structure, elevated above a dual carriageway. Across the town, pedestrians were conscientiously partitioned from cars. Footpaths were laid out above or under, but never alongside, the fast-flowing expressways that made up Cumbernauld's hierarchical road system. A network of these walkways connected the town centre to the housing, so that pedestrians need never come in contact with vehicles.[50]

The ambitious concept soon received international critical acclaim; the Institute of American Architects, for example, selected the town centre as the best building in the world. However, it was not long before the realities of daily life set in. The hilltop site was little liked by residents, who faced a steep, windswept walk to the complex. Its grey concrete surfaces were painted white to temper its foreboding appearance, yet still, the town centre was left unvisited. Residents got in their cars and drove elsewhere, thereby exacerbating the pattern of suburban life that its planners had wanted to combat.[51] Cumbernauld, the great modernist utopia, quickly came to be regarded as a brutalist carbuncle.

Much of the architecture realised as part of the New Towns programme has come to be derided. Whether at East Kilbride, Cumbernauld, or the two later Scottish towns, Livingstone (designated 1962) and Irvine (designated 1966), the mass scale and pace at which construction took place meant squeezed budgets, standardisation

Above /
Cumbernauld, founded in
1956 and planned from 1958,
prioritised higher density than
the earlier New Towns through
tighter clustering of housing
grouped around a central area.

of units, untried materials and large blocks, which are now inherently inflexible and weathering badly with age. Edward Jones, one of the architects of the Netherfield estate in Milton Keynes (designated 1967), has reflected that planners and architects rushed to break free from the past, but 'with little understanding of the nature of place that would result'.[52] Nevertheless, it must be remembered that the New Towns were products of their post-war age. They belonged to an era of optimism, of the 'brave new world', when British society was unanimous in its self-belief that it could solve the problems of old towns and cities. Visualisations of spacious sunlit houses, tower blocks, schools and shopping centres chimed deeply with a generation then living with bombed-out nineteenth-century streets.

Taken as a whole, the New Towns programme was a herculean undertaking; it amounts to the largest public house building scheme ever attempted. By 1991, one in 25 of all new dwellings constructed in the UK since 1945 was built within a New Town.[53] Boasting comparatively modest levels of outward commuting, the towns were hugely effectual in fulfilling the objective of decentralising residents and industry away from Britain's major conurbations. The places thus created now play home to over two million people, and they continue to grow. Still, though, they cannot shake off a reputation for monotone architecture, dormitory suburbs and car dependency. As exemplified at Cumbernauld, the towns' generous accommodation for the car and emphatic separation of foot from vehicular traffic tended to counter the desire to create genuine communities and instead formed 'the starting point in the UK for the car-based urbanism that has since become the norm'.[54] As early as 1954, Lewis Mumford critiqued the low density of the New Towns, which left their neighbourhoods 'too widely scattered to fulfil the social purposes of living together

in an urban community'.[55] In their overt rejection of traditional town patterns, the New Towns had little of the social urban activity that fostered community spirit. 'A lack of humanity, warmth or spark of life in public places is perhaps the most telling characteristic of too many British new towns', concluded the *Washington Post* in 1972.[56]

SCOTLAND'S NEW URBANISM

By the end of the 1970s, Westminster's fervour for the New Towns movement was waning. The spiralling economic decline of the UK's inner cities was increasingly gaining prominence and, come 1980, a major shift in policy saw decentralisation supplanted by urban regeneration. State-funded construction came to a near standstill, and house-building rates plummeted. Local authorities stopped investing in new building and the private sector did not make up the deficit. While building levels slowed, the rate of household formation, however, did not. Consequently, the UK has been chronically underbuilding since the 1980s. Scotland has seen the annual number of new dwellings fall from 36,029 in 1966, to 21,281 in 1996, down to 16,953 in 2016.[57]

The development that has occurred in recent years has typically been undertaken by large, volume house builders as extensions to existing towns. All too frequently, it takes the form of sprawling, monocultural housing. 'Too much development in Scotland is a missed opportunity and of mediocre or indifferent quality', concluded the 2008 report of the Council of Economic Advisers to the Scottish Government. 'There are a few examples of new or regenerated places which are well thought out... but they are the exception rather than the rule.'[58]

In the current climate of scarcity, though, even the most undistinguished developments sell. Armed with this information, there is little incentive for volume builders to aspire to good design. Most new housing schemes are carried forth on a basis by which the developer does not have a long-term financial interest in the site, and thus cannot command the rewards that high-quality urbanism returns in the long run; neither does he bear the price of bad design. The priority is to build swiftly, efficiently, then move onto the next project. Although written in 2007, the verdict drawn by the Callcutt Review of Housebuilding Delivery continues to be germane:

> Housebuilders must build to meet regulatory and warranty standards. But in a market which does not offer a cost effective return for higher quality, there is little incentive for them to go further; and many do not... Their first duty is to their investors, and if the best returns are to be achieved with little regard to quality beyond minimum standards, so be it.[59]

Yet, the situation is not wholly bleak. Enthusiasm has been growing in the UK for an alternative model to large-scale suburban expansion, one that seeks a return to what can loosely be termed 'traditional urbanism' – and Scotland has been at the spearhead of this trend. It has its roots in the 1980s, when two kindred movements – New Urbanism in North America and Urban Villages in Europe – kindled a rapprochement with historic urban patterns. Disaffected with the aesthetic, environmental and social repercussions of the rampant suburbanisation of the twentieth century, a new generation of architects, planners and critics sought an antidote. Their approach rejected modernism – which, they argued, used the city as a forum for experimentation – and reappropriated the essentials of timeless urbanism that had shaped towns prior to the dominance of the car.

Much of the impetus behind the revival came from the Belgian urban theorist, Leon Krier. Recoiling against aberrations of post-war development within Europe's historic towns and cities, Krier's methodology involves distilling the traditional building blocks of city design, the mainstay of which is the 'urban quarter'. Krier puts forward the urban quarter as the basis for a reformed urbanism of the present age. Each quarter has a prescribed boundary and distinct centre, and contains a range of housing, workplaces, education and leisure facilities linked by a pedestrian network to permit of a full community life. Krier's neo-rationalist discourse inspired practitioners in the US, notably Andrés Duany, Elizabeth Plater-Zyberk and Peter Calthorpe, who collectively established the New Urbanism movement as an agency of anti-sprawl.

The New Urbanist agenda champions the concept of the 'neighbourhood unit' as the backbone of town building. Challenging the modernist tendency to subdivide land into single-use zones, its exponents seek a return to compact, mixed-use development comprising a full spectrum of housing types, schools, shops, workplaces and other activities connected by a pedestrian nexus. Design principles emphasising higher-than-average densities, mass transit over cars, green space and sensitivity to local topography and climate are advocated as a means of achieving more sustainable and legible urban environments, whilst, furthermore, fostering community life within them.[60] Kentlands in Maryland (master planned by DPZ, begun 1988) was one of the earliest New Urbanist projects to be built. Six neighbourhoods were set out around a town centre, featuring a cultural hub, shops and offices. A prime objective of the design was that retail be connected to the neighbourhoods' street network, fostering pedestrian activity within and across the districts. A mixture of housing types was constructed to promote diversity of residents, while houses themselves were built with minimum setbacks from the street and upon smaller plots to achieve residential compactness and thus encourage sociability amongst neighbours. [61] New Urbanism's advocates share a core raison d'être: the improvement of civic life through design. 'We realise that physical solutions by themselves will not solve social and economic problems', affirms the Charter of the Congress of New Urbanism, 'but neither can economic vitality, community stability, and environmental health be sustained without a coherent and supportive physical framework.' It is tempting to see parallels with the Enlightenment doctrine of the Age of Improvers.

The approach is not without its critics. Some have questioned the real sustainability value of the schemes. Alex Marshall, for example, points to the lack of retail in Celebration in Florida, one of New Urbanism's best known outputs, which forces residents to drive elsewhere for even supermarket essentials.[62] The most divisive issue surrounding New Urbanism, though, is one of aesthetics. The Charter of the Congress of New Urbanism firmly steers import away from architectural style in favour of spatial structure; it emphasises that design should take its cues from the history, building and landscape traditions of the locality. Yet in practice, many New Urbanism developments have a traditional face and, much to the chagrin of some of its practitioners, this has come to outwardly characterise the movement.[63]

The traditional architectural forms are typically upheld through strict design codes. Again, this echoes controls enforced by the eighteenth-century Improvers. Kentlands' architecture, for example, has been the subject of rigid controls at both design and execution. Its 'Design Standards' mandates that exterior walls must be of brick, stone, smooth stucco or timber; window frames be wooden; roofs be gables and hips, pitched between 9:12 and 14:12; and that walls that are constructed of more than one medium should only change material along a horizontal line, and not a vertical or diagonal one. These guidelines not only governed what the original builders could do, but also any additions or alterations that homeowners can make. New Urbanism's perceived fealty to traditional idioms and exacting design codes has alienated many outside the movement. To the professional mainstream in particular, the implication that the past holds more value than the present represents a direct challenge to contemporary innovation.[64]

Detractors aside, the New Urbanism and Urban Village movements have gained traction as an important alternative to the post-war norms of low-density, car-dominant development. In Britain, the most vehement adherent to this ideology has been the Prince of Wales. In 1993, he famously put into practice his conviction

Above ╱
Poundbury, an urban
extension to Dorchester
begun in 1993 as a test
bed for compact, mixed-
use development with
pedestrian priority.

that traditional mixed-use developments are the most sustainable path for urban
expansion by commencing the construction of Poundbury, a 162-hectare settlement
on Duchy of Cornwall-owned land in Dorset. Meanwhile, the movement has been
endorsed by other high-profile figures. Then Deputy Prime Minister John Prescott
argued for a 'new vision of what we mean by sustainable communities – what the
Americans call "New Urbanism"' when speaking at the 2002 Urban Summit in
Manchester. George Ferguson used his 2003-5 presidency of the Royal Institute
of British Architects to push for a new urbanism in a UK context, enjoining
practitioners to design 'truly mixed-use communities'.[65]

It is, though, in Scotland that traditional urbanism has been most comprehensively
and coherently embraced within the British Isles. Since the turn of the millennium,
the Scottish Government has embarked upon a reformist agenda, seeking to
improve the quality of places through the issuance of policy guidance and design
initiatives. 'The Development of a Policy on Architecture for Scotland' (1999)
launched the dialogue by advocating the importance of planning with regard to
the urban traditions and landscapes of Scotland; 'Designing Streets' (2010) was
efficacious in marking a new direction in official guidance on street design away
from a system built around the primacy of cars and towards place-making; and the
Scottish Sustainable Communities Initiative (initiated in 2008) encouraged higher
standards of housing-led developments at 11 exemplar sites, notably through three,
week-long public design workshops led by Andrés Duany in 2010. New Urbanist
concepts have thus been elevated in official policy, but they have not remained
merely theoretical. A number of new settlements and urban extensions are being
built or in the process of being planned that can be grouped under the traditional

urbanism banner. These include Tornagrain, a 4,960-home town east of Inverness being pursued by the Earl of Moray; Grandhome, a 4,700-unit urban extension to Aberdeen; and Chapelton.

That they are actually being realised has much to do with patterns of land ownership in Scotland. The country has a high number of large, family-controlled estates compared with the rest of the UK, and the involvement of many of these families in the creation of new settlements during the eighteenth and nineteenth centuries sets an ideological precedent that should not be underestimated. Take Tornagrain as an example. When the Highland Council opened discussions with the Earl of Moray in the early 2000s about using part of his estate to absorb the region's anticipated population growth, his engagement with the idea owed much to the Moray family's ancestral involvement in town planning at Edinburgh New Town. It is no coincidence that the current generation of traditional urbanist schemes is being propelled by the likes of the Earl of Moray and Duke of Fife. They have long-running concerns in the sites. Tornagrain, for instance, is being built on land that has been owned by the Earl of Moray's ancestors since the sixteenth century. This vested interest in the estate sets him squarely apart from a standard developer who, as a generalisation, thinks of land on a short-term basis as an asset to be exploited quickly and cost-effectively. The Earl of Moray is prepared to take an extended, measured view, and appreciates the premium that highly crafted construction and well-considered urbanism will reap over time.

It was, in fact, Lord Moray who first brought Duany to the UK after being approached by the Highland Council. Discontented with the low-quality sprawl that had crept across the Highlands in recent decades, he decided to take the lead by planning and developing a new town on 200 hectares of his land identified by the Council. It would, he determined, counter prevalent patterns of single-use, car-dominated housing developments by taking inspiration from places like Grantown-on-Spey and Inverary to embody the best lessons of traditional Scottish urbanism. This aspiration took him to Miami-based Duany and his practice DPZ, known for its sensitive and context-driven approach to design. He not only engaged DPZ to master plan Tornagrain in 2006, but also brought Duany to Britain to deliver three public lectures about the New Urbanism methodology. It was through Duany's 2006 visit that Jim McKinnon, then Chief Planner for Scotland, and John Swinney, later Finance Secretary, became enthused to actively promote traditional urbanism using such mechanisms as the Scottish Sustainable Communities Initiative.

Tornagrain was, thus, at the forefront of the trend. Yet it is Knockroon in East Ayrshire that can lay claim to being the first built demonstration of Scotland's new urbanism. Construction began on the 28-hectare site, purchased by the Prince of Wales following his acquisition of nearby Dumfries House, in 2011. It has been planned as a neighbourhood extension to Cumnock, a sixteenth-century burgh, comprising 770 homes, local shops and workplaces for small businesses.

Above /
Tornagrain, a 5,000-home
new town under construction
near Inverness, engages
New Urbanist philosophy
in reaction to the spread
of suburban sprawl across
the Highlands.

The two schemes share a set of defining principles, which encapsulate traditional urbanism as a whole: they combine a mix of uses; they are pedestrian friendly; they elevate time-tested values of town making and spatial structure; and they are born of a plan-making process that promotes public participation. They are also strongly driven by the overall vision of their landowners. Echoing the architectural guidelines enjoined by the city council for Edinburgh New Town or James Grant for Grantown-on-Spey, this generation of landowners uses pattern books or design codes to ensure that their aspirations are upheld. Knockroon's design code, for example, sets out detailed rules for all aspects of its environment, from the boundary wall materials to road widths, to the ratio of windows to walls on houses. The specifications are based upon a rigorous study of vernacular precedents in East Ayrshire and the west of Scotland. The terrace housing forming the town edge that fronts the main road derives from a model in Lanark, for instance, whilst the border facing the countryside is based upon housing typologies at the fringe of Mauchline. Drawing on the regional vernacular is an established New Urbanist practice to foster meaningful identities within new settlements, but Knockroon's designers have rendered their eighteenth- and nineteenth-century precedents with particular fidelity and discernment. There is no overwrought historicism in its plainspoken, regularly fronted cottages.

Much of the historic fabric of Scotland's cities, towns and villages is simple in style, and the overall charm of their streetscapes derives as much from the spatial structures as architecture. The diversity of squares, streets, wynds, pends and closes brings a richness of character that the bland homogeneity of much new residential building does not even come close to, but which schemes like Knockroon, Tornagrain and Chapelton are informed by.

The built output of this new wave of urbanism is relatively modest; many proposals
remain on the drawing board. Building in the twenty-first century entails logistics
and legalities that the Enlightenment Improvers did not have to contend with.
Yet they are on track to make an important contribution to the history of planned
town creation in Scotland. This new generation of settlements are the royal burghs
or planned villages of the modern age. They can be viewed as part of a long and
distinguished history of planned town creation that sets Scotland apart from the
rest of the British Isles. With high points in the Middle Ages and the Enlightenment,
the country has an established culture of deliberately founding and planning new
places to answer specific objectives. Many of the communities thus created are
amongst its most admired and enduring environments today. With the prototypes
of Chapelton, Tornagrain and their peers, there is the potential for another layer to
be added to this remarkable legacy of planned towns. ◆

CHAPTER TWO
THE MAKING OF CHAPELTON

As sketched in the previous pages, Scotland has a long and distinctive tradition in the planning of new towns. Chapelton is the newest chapter in this story. It is a pioneer of a new approach to designing and building our urban environment, and it is undertaking it at a scale unprecedented in the North East. Chapelton has the potential to become the largest town in the Aberdeenshire Council area. And yet its founders never set out with a fixed intention to realise a new town at all.

The source of the project can be traced back to a road, the Aberdeen Western Peripheral Route (AWPR). The construction of this long-anticipated carriageway – the first plan dates back to 1948 – was announced by the First Minister in 2003 to improve travel in the north east of Scotland by providing an additional route from north to south Aberdeen that bypasses the city. In 2007, the fourth Duke of Fife (then Earl of Southesk) learnt that an 11.5-kilometre stretch of the road was being designed to pass along the western edge of the Elsick estate, a 630-hectare property that had been owned by his family for generations. The news prompted him to take stock and question what this meant for the land as a whole. It was then that he discovered that preparations were underway by Aberdeen City and Aberdeenshire Councils for a structure plan for the area and that this had the potential for far-reaching ramifications for Elsick. The draft plan, which was published in 2008, proposed a huge amount of housing – 72,000 new homes as well as associated infrastructure and employment land – to be built over the next two decades in three strategic growth areas, one of which encompassed the land on which Chapelton sits. 'It seemed quite clear', recalled The Duke of Fife, 'that a huge amount of housing was going to appear on our doorstep'.[01]

Speculative builders lost little time in approaching him about purchasing land. The family, though, recoiled at the recent precedents of volume building in the North East. The area had long suffered from a lack of long-term thinking; suburban sprawl populated by mediocre housing had inch-by-inch spread across Aberdeenshire, too limited in scale to enable sufficient facilities to sustain any true community. It was a fate that they did not want to see for the Elsick estate. 'We took the view quickly', recollected the Duke,

> that if it was going to happen all around us and the area was going to change dramatically, we might as well go for what I call the 'nuclear option' – a major-scale development on the estate and a full-scale project rather than death by a thousand cuts around the edges.
> It wasn't a deliberate idea to build a town, it was much more circumstantial than that.[02]

Thus the idea to build Chapelton was born. The Elsick Development Company (EDC), with the future fourth Duke and Duchess as directors, was incorporated on 20 August 2008 and the company submitted a bid to Aberdeenshire Council for the estate to be included as a prospective site within its forthcoming Local Development Plan (LDP).

Above /
The open farmland that
comprised the Chapelton
site prior to development.

The Elsick estate comprised several small clusters of houses, including the hamlet from which Chapelton takes its name, but the majority was agricultural fields. With views to the North Sea, it is a naturally beautiful slice of gently rolling Aberdeenshire countryside. As farmland, though, it has never been very productive. Statistical accounts from the eighteenth and nineteenth centuries disclose that those living off the land struggled for every crust; there are places on the site where the shallow soil and rocky underlayers make it impossible to get a plough in the ground. If open farmland is going to be given over to development, one can reason, it may as well be low-yielding land such as this. Its topography also makes the estate an apt fit for large-scale development. The site occupies a natural bowl and low, rounded ridges to the north, south and west effectively screen it from much of the surrounding area.

To further improve the site's potential as a location for a new settlement in terms of position, terrain and size, the EDC entered into a consortium with four neighbouring farmers to expand the Elsick property by 210 hectares, making a total of 840 hectares. The consortium contract was structured so that the four farmers bear no risk in the venture and the EDC retains control over the way the development unfolds.

The next step was to open discussions with house builders and consultants. This the EDC did, becoming after months of negotiations close to an agreement with two builders and going as far as to select a planning practice and urban designer. By this time, however, the impact of the global financial crisis was spreading throughout the country. Notwithstanding that the Aberdeen housing market was still booming

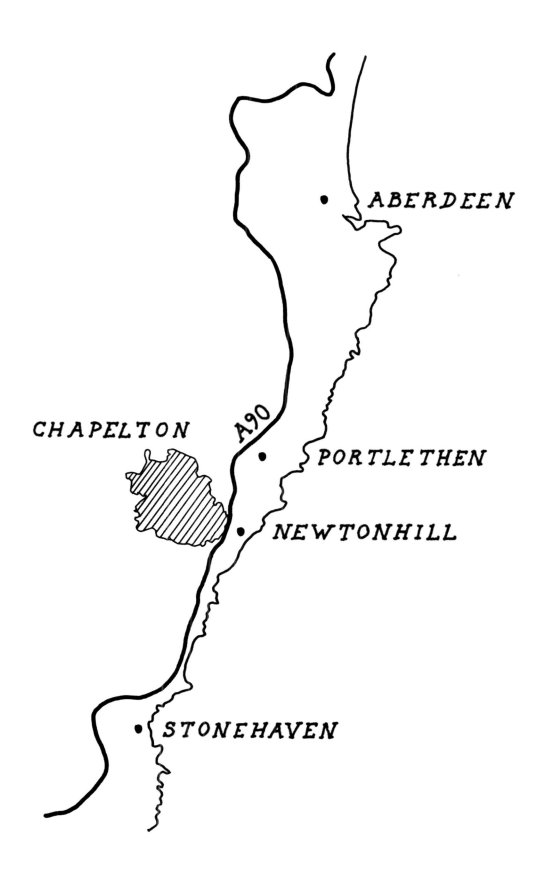

ABERDEEN

CHAPELTON

A90

PORTLETHEN

NEWTONHILL

STONEHAVEN

thanks to its oil industry, the UK construction sector came grinding to a near halt. With finance scarce and mortgage availability limited, house builders were placed under enormous strain. The two aforementioned builders changed their terms so dramatically that they were now unviable. The EDC returned to the drawing board.

Therefore, while best-laid plans were apparently tumbling, it was, conversely, about this time that the Duke and Duchess got their first official indication that their vision might actually lead somewhere. In May 2009, Aberdeenshire Council published its Main Issues Report (MIR), identifying its preferred development sites to be included within the LDP. The MIR determined the need for 4,600 additional homes between Portlethen and Stonehaven by 2023 and suggested that the best means of addressing this challenge would be the development of a new settlement. It named two potential sites: Banchory Leggart, just south of Aberdeen, and Elsick.

After nearly a year of public consultation, in March 2010 the Kincardine and Mearns Special Area Committee convened to debate the MIR's recommendations. Although the Committee quickly agreed to adopt the strategy for a new settlement, the question remained as to where it should be built. The Aberdeenshire Council planning officers advocated that the Banchory Leggart site was the best option for answering the locality's growth needs. It was, they argued, easier to deliver in the short term and would have less impact on the transport system. However, its great drawback was that the site was too constrained to meet the full housing target; it would require 1,550 houses to be built on a separate parcel of land to the north of Portlethen. This is where Elsick had its major advantage. Over the previous year, the Duke had canvassed council meetings and met with local interest groups to express his vision for a coherent, long-term plan that could accommodate all the area's growth for the forthcoming decades. Drawing attention to Aberdeenshire's recent history of endless urban extensions and lack of an overarching development strategy, he presented the Elsick estate as the most rational, far-sighted and sustainable option for development. The 12 members of the Committee unanimously voted to allot all the locality's housing to Elsick. It was a plucky move on behalf of the councillors: the EDC was new to the business, neither did it have house builders in place. Nonetheless, from that moment, Chapelton took a step closer to becoming a reality.

The Committee's decision sparked a period of intense activity. Keen to capture the momentum of this advocacy, the Duke and Duchess sought to work quickly. This was easier said than done, however; neither had any experience in the field of large-scale development. And so they turned for advice to family friend and distant cousin, the Earl of Moray, who had initiated his own plans for a new town, Tornagrain, near Inverness several years earlier (see page 35).

The Earl of Moray had taken an approach then completely novel in the UK. He had engaged Miami-based practice DPZ, led by Andrés Duany, to master plan a comprehensive, pedestrian-orientated settlement informed by the New Urbanist precepts that Duany had helped to pioneer. This was an adventurous step on his part; DPZ had never before worked in the UK. Yet, the firm had designed over 300 communities elsewhere across the world, driven by an aspiration to counter ad hoc suburban sprawl with a return to the principles of traditional town building. Furthermore, it is credited with the development of the 'charrette' as a vehicle for design and public engagement.

The term charrette, derived from the French for 'cart', refers to the intense surge of activity undertaken by architects prior to a deadline. Lore has it that it derives from the nineteenth-century practice at the École des Beaux-Arts in Paris, whereby a cart was circulated to collect students' drawings and models. The students, frantically working until the last moment, would jump onto the wagon to add final touches to their work even whilst it was being wheeled away. Today, a charrette refers to a fast-paced workshop where design professionals, key decision makers and the lay community are brought together to develop a master plan in a limited time frame.

The method has several distinct attractions. By assembling architects, planners, engineers, local residents, councillors, transport officials and others, a charrette correlates all the component parts of a complex project quickly and efficiently. Concepts can be swiftly discussed, reviewed and decided upon, saving months of sequential planning. Moreover, it is an effective vehicle for obtaining public input and forging shared local interest in the scheme. Open public meetings, presentations and drop-in studio sessions shape the charrette process, allowing attendees the opportunity to influence the master plan, either by suggesting ideas or identifying concerns. This is in pronounced contrast to conventional consultation mechanisms in the UK, whereby the public is only invited to comment after the design work has been done.

The Duke and Duchess of Fife promptly perceived the advantages of DPZ's working approach to their situation. They were keenly aware that, although the Special Area Committee had voted in their favour, they would inevitably be heavily challenged about their capability to deliver such a large development. DPZ's method was, they perceived, a means to steal a march on competitors and critics. By undertaking a charrette exercise immediately, they could substantially accelerate the design, analysis and planning process and thereby, they hoped, lock the Elsick estate into the Local Development Plan that was then being prepared. Pursing this route was a financial gamble; there was no certainty that any master plan thus designed would be adopted by the Council. Nonetheless, within weeks the EDC appointed DPZ to master plan the site, and London-based Turnberry Consulting, which had also worked at Tornagrain, to manage the design and delivery channels.

In late September of the same year, an eleven-strong DPZ team swapped Florida sunshine for the Aberdeenshire countryside to commence a 10-day charrette. Joined by ecology experts, engineers, landscape designers and architects from Aberdeenshire and further afield, they set up camp in the indoor swimming pool

of Elsick House, the thirteenth-century home at the centre of the estate. The pool house was transformed into a temporary design studio open to members of the public for the duration of the event. Extensive preparation had already been undertaken in the preceding weeks, including topographical studies, landscape reports and reviews of north-east Scotland's architectural and urban traditions, which provided indispensible groundwork for the team during the charrette. Those 10 days were ones of intense activity. Dozens of iterations of the master plan were advanced, gradually shaping the urban form in line with the contours of the site, whilst specialist groups gathered to debate specific elements of the plan.

The master plan's evolution was strongly influenced by the contributions and commentary from the surrounding community. In the run up to the charrette, the EDC held a public meeting and delivered 5,000 pamphlets across the area to publicise and encourage participation in the event. The degree to which the locals engaged with and supported the project, though, exceeded all expectations. Some 560 people attended the charrette, notably at the opening, mid-term and closing presentations held in nearby Newtonhill. 'From the charrette process, you really find that listening to local people is a very helpful way to learn what is lacking in the area', recalled the Duchess.[03] In the case of Chapelton, feedback during the charrette led to the incorporation of a body of water for kayaking, a bicycle route suggested by keen cyclists and the reworking of some areas of the development to accommodate existing properties. The design team held specific sessions to address the concerns of neighbouring homeowners. 'We went into the charrette with a certain amount of nervousness about how people would view proposals', said The Duke of Fife.

> Large development is seldom very popular, but the great thing about the charrette process is that it eliminates any bitterness. People know you have heard what they have to say. Locals were in large measure supportive of what we were setting out to achieve. It was gratifying to learn through the discussions we had with them that they didn't want the alternative: their small towns and villages being systematically extended. And, mistrustful of conventional house builders and developers, they viewed the family's involvement as a level of quality control that they had faith in.[04]

During the charrette, plans were constantly modified based on the comments and critiques from the public and professionals, and by the close of the 10 days, the design team had developed a long-term, high-level blueprint for the entire 840 hectares. Anticipated to ultimately house 8,000 dwellings, the plan structured the town into a network of seven neighbourhoods plus a town centre, to be built in phases as the population grows. Inspired by a fusion of historic regional town precedents and DPZ's New Urbanist philosophy, the layout was compact and mixed-use, with shops, parks and schools within walking distance of all residences. Diagrams identifying the nexus of open space, cycle routes and thoroughfare network were also produced during the charrette, as were illustrations of bird's-eye views and street-level perspectives. 'Over 10 days, I think we achieved 18 months of work', said The Duke of Fife. 'Because you've got the whole team there, you can get decisions made and move on quickly.'[05]

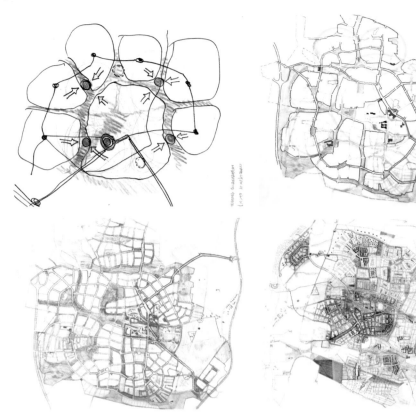

Above /
Evolution of the master plan. During
the charrette, the plan was constantly
modified based on comments and
critiques from the local community
and specialists.

Right /
Chapelton's master plan (2011), a
blue print for the town's long-term
development comprising up to 8,000
homes structured within seven
neighbourhoods.

The sheer volume of work produced during the charrette was to prove pivotal in
subsequent months in securing Chapelton's place within the Aberdeenshire LDP.
When the Directorate of Planning and Environmental Appeals (DPEA) conducted a
hearing session in October 2011 on behalf of the Scottish Government to adjudicate
Chapelton's place in the draft plan, the EDC had some 2,000 pages of well-prepared
documentation to support its position. Other developers called into question
the EDC's ability to deliver the scheme given its inexperience and the size of the
settlement, but the depth and scope of this dossier set Chapelton far ahead of any
rival proposals and invested the DPEA Reporter with the confidence to endorse its
inclusion within the LDP.[06]

This, however, is jumping ahead of time. To return to the months succeeding the
charrette, this was a period of fine-tuning and financial analysis as the team worked
towards submitting a planning application. Brooks Murray Architects – whose
director, Gavin Murray, grew up in Aberdeen – was appointed town architect and
travelled to Miami for a mini design workshop held at DPZ's studio in December
2010. Meanwhile, the EDC continued to meet with community groups, and staged
public exhibitions in the nearby hamlet of Cookney in March and June 2011 to
illustrate the subsequent evolution of the plan.

The pace of progress was swift. In September 2011, less than a year after the closing of the charrette, the EDC submitted two planning applications to Aberdeenshire Council. The first was an outline application for the initial 4,045 homes[07] and the second was a detailed application for 802 homes within the first neighbourhood, Cairnhill. Submitting such a large detailed application was an unusual but deliberate move. In the months after the charrette, the EDC, DPZ and the wider team asked themselves a question: if they approached the Scottish house-building market with the Chapelton master plan, would the built product align with the vision? The conclusion they arrived at was, probably not. Chapelton is aspiring towards a type and quality of environment that most twenty-first-century house builders are simply not used to delivering. The solution they arrived at was twofold. Firstly, the EDC would bind itself to a detailed planning submission that would set the measure for the first neighbourhood: a mix of residential properties, business units and open space; a range of street hierarchies; and architecture and urbanism informed by regional precedents. Secondly, it undertook to install the initial infrastructure – roads, sewerage, water – itself. This was an expensive decision – it entailed an investment of some £9 million – but it meant that the EDC would not be incumbent upon a developer to put the infrastructure in place and thereby it would retain absolute control of the overall direction of the scheme and its quality.

For the next two years, the EDC, Turnberry Consulting and the design team were consumed by complex planning, infrastructure and commercial discussions. For those involved, after the celerity of the previous 18 months, progress often seemed almost painfully fraught. Aside from negotiating with the statutory authorities, they also began the search for house builders. This in itself was no mean feat. The Duke and Duchess of Fife determined to use Aberdeenshire firms wherever possible, but most local developers struggled to understand the Chapelton philosophy. Equally, national volume developers had little interest in undertaking any form of bespoke development that deviated from their standard offering. After an exacting hunt and in-depth talks to ensure that they grasped the Chapelton vision, the EDC entered into agreements with three contractors: ZeroC, which had worked at Poundbury and thus was familiar with the precepts of traditional urbanism; AJC Homes, an Aberdeenshire boutique house builder; and Perth-based A & J Stephen, a family firm established in 1935.

On 30 April 2013, the Kincardine and Mearns Area Committee resolved to grant planning permission for Chapelton, but it was not until five months later, on 2 October, that the Aberdeenshire Provost hand delivered the planning permission sealed in a brown envelope, the very same day that ground was finally broken during a foundation ceremony. W. M. Donald, the Aberdeenshire-based engineering contractor, was in situ to commence the enormous task of embedding essential infrastructure – the roads, drainage and services that make up the backbone of any town – into the farmland site. Construction started at the edge of the Cairnhill neighbourhood, close to the A90. It would have made little sense to begin with the town centre before the settlement was sufficiently populated, and so building was phased to commence with 256 houses centred around Greenlaw Road, the approach into Chapelton from the east, and Hume Square, the site of its first neighbourhood green and shops.

Nearly every detail of construction, from the road design to the architecture to the public realm, was governed by the Chapelton Design Framework. This is discussed in more detail in the next chapter, but essentially it is a suite of documents prepared to ensure the town is developed in line with the EDC vision by providing detailed guidance on street, block and building designs. While ZeroC was familiar with working with very defined design regulations, having experienced something similar at Poundbury, the other two house builders were initially apprehensive about the level of control, chary of its apparent prescriptiveness. 'Every house builder had their own individual preferences, built up over years of experience', reflected Gavin Murray, 'and in many matters we were asking them to turn these on their head, taking them back to much more traditional precedents.'[08]

To arrive at a formula that all the house builders were in agreement with took time. 'There was a discrepancy between what the design team wanted, and what we could build and sell', Alistair Aboyne of AJC Homes reflected.[09] A cycle of dialogue and revision between Brooks Murray and the three house builders took place to achieve a situation where all were content. In many respects, this cycle will continue throughout the build, although it becomes quicker with familiarity. 'The house builders would admittedly probably still prefer the freedom to build their own designs', continued Murray, 'but they understand the long-term potential of the site and accept why we take this unified approach. The initial fear that a design code would be limiting and cause delays is now accepted as a means of ensuring Chapelton's built output and its future quality.'[10]

Creating a place that diverges from the norms of twenty-first-century house building and urban design has brought its teething problems. Contractors were tasked with meeting specifications that they had never tackled before. No firm in Scotland, it transpired, had practical knowledge of how to run metal rims along grass verges, for example, and the contractor struggled at first to master the practice. With time, this and other arts have been acquired, although inevitably it has been a consuming drain on resources.

Managing relations with Aberdeenshire Council and other statutory authorities has also been a learning curve. 'Overwhelmingly, the Council officials are supportive of what we are trying to achieve', The Duchess of Fife avers. 'They must be praised for having the farsightedness to sanction a development so far removed from conventional models. Yet, they find the aspects of the project that are outside of their previous experience extremely difficult to accommodate at the beginning.'[11] Pursuing historic urban patterns and vernacular materials within the current regulatory environment has proven an exhausting challenge for the wider Chapelton team. The common proviso, for instance, that roads be wide enough to

accommodate the turn of a refuse lorry is at odds with the human-scaled hierarchy of street widths that is part of the natural rhythm of old towns; it is antithetical to recreating the types of back lanes and wynds that are distinctive of many Scottish towns, cities and villages. Similarly, new properties that open directly onto the street are frowned upon, because they entail house foundations being built underneath pavements, despite this model being a common sight across north-east Scotland.

Nationwide, twenty-first century approaches to new development have become standardised, to the extent that features familiar to historic urban environments, such as wall-mounted street lights or granite kerbs, are now deemed aberrant within many official directives. At Chapelton, for example, the use of granite setts, inspired by precedents in Aberdeen, or the drystone wall on the approach road (plate II) into the town were considered 'non-standard details' by Aberdeenshire Council. This is despite the historic importance of the granite industry to Aberdeen and the frequency of drystone walls within the surrounding countryside. The issue is not unique to Aberdeenshire Council. Shrinking budgets mean that local authorities want streetscapes that are easy to maintain at the lowest cost to them. This stance, though, is frequently inimical with good place-making.

The laborious complexity of delivering environments that deviate from the mainstream language of housing estates explains why there are not more Chapeltons being built in the UK; nearly all conventional developers would simply give up in frustration. The fact that Chapelton does have drystone walls, granite setts, back lanes and so forth is testimony to the tenacity of the team and the long-termism of The Duke and Duchess of Fife. In theory, the process is getting easier –

a 'non-standard detail' needs only to be approved once, but reaching that stage is onerous and time consuming. 'One of the problems', according to the Duke, 'is that we are the first to fully take on traditional urbanism in Aberdeenshire. When you're the first one into the game, it's a very slow business.'[12]

The years since the project began have been a learning process for everyone involved. Amongst the sharpest lessons has been the volatility of the property market. At the time when construction started, Aberdeen was at the height of a property boom. While the rest of the country was reeling from the effects of the 2008 recession, high oil prices created a North Sea energy bubble in the city and its vicinity. House prices in Aberdeen more than doubled in the decade up to 2014, reaching almost 50 per cent above the Scottish mean. However, the global collapse in the value of oil in 2014 led to a dramatic reversal in fortune. As the oil industry cut thousands of jobs, Aberdeen became Britain's worst-performing property market. Between 2014 and 2017, home prices fell by an average of 10 per cent.

The slump in the market has had a palpable effect upon Chapelton's rate of progress. The initial high sales tally following the opening of sales in May 2014 decelerated and the house builders slowed their rate of construction in response. In many ways, Chapelton was fortunate; if it had launched two years later, it may not have been able to weather the storm. Still, the downturn has proven frustrating not only financially, but also in terms of achieving the EDC's vision of a holistic, sustainable community. Without sufficient volume of occupied houses, there can be no schools, no GP practice, no supermarket. It is only when residents can access these and other daily needs within a short walk of their home that Chapelton will fulfil its objectives. 'New Urbanism requires a pretty complete package to deliver the walkable lifestyle', the Duke observed, 'so the quicker things go, the better things go.'[13] Even in this difficult market place, though, development has continued, slowly but surely. The three house builders, confident in the fundamental merit of the product, have resisted lowering specifications or slashing house prices, as a volume builder might, simply to achieve magnitude of sales. 'We are all in it for the long term', said Aboyne of the three firms. 'We want to maintain the vision and uphold the value of properties going forward and properties we have already sold.'[14]

Nonetheless, the changes in the housing market have resulted in subtle changes to the town's master plan. The most demonstrable of these is on Farquharson Street, where eight four-bedroom, detached houses were replaced by 20 two-bedroom, single-storey cottages (completed 2018) arranged around three courts, reflecting the wane in demand for large houses. Nearby, a block overlooking Liddell Park that was previously designated as purely residential has been altered to house a retirement village (scheduled completion 2019). Featuring fitness facilities, a restaurant and nearly 100 flats and cottages exclusively for the over-55s, the model fits well with Chapelton's 'whole-of-life' ethos. However, its addition to the master plan was adopted as a strategy to keep development moving forward; the retirement market sector is one of the few in Aberdeen not directly impacted by the oil industry.

Inevitably, the master plan has evolved. Chapelton is a four-decade-long project, and DPZ's high-level blueprint produced in 2010 was never conceived to be an ossified formula. As work progresses, improvements are identified and implemented by Brooks Murray. The ability to make these changes is indicative of the flexibility of the development model. For example, if the site was being advanced by a conventional volume builder whose product did not usually include retirement complexes, then the concept of the retirement village at Liddell Park would simply never have been contemplated. The Duke of Fife is conscious, though, that any changes must align with the spirit of the master plan that was presented to local residents and the wider public. The pledges made then must be upheld to retain popular faith that Chapelton is a breed apart from conventional developments.

There are numerous citable examples that identify how the EDC at Chapelton is deliberately steering a different course to standard developers, not only in its espousal of traditional urbanism but also in the heed paid to off-site and on-site residents. For instance, to ensure Chapelton inhabitants and those in the existing neighbouring clusters of houses at Windyedge and Cammachmore do not have a constant stream of site traffic passing their front doors, the EDC has built haul roads to divert construction vehicles.

More remarkable, though, has been the solicitude given to building a sense of community within the fledgling settlement. One of the first tangible manifestations of Chapelton was Teacake, a café housed initially within a temporary cabin at the entrance to the town and, from October 2015, at a permanent location in Hume Square. It is not a profit-making venture for the EDC, yet The Duchess of Fife has averred that having Teacake 'was the best thing we ever did. Homebuyers would visit the site to see progress on their house, drop in for a cup of tea and chat to others who would also be moving in.'[15] It was the formation of the community before the physical reality had occurred. A nursery soon opened alongside it in Hume Square, followed by a hair and beauty salon in November 2016. A typical volume builder in the UK would reason such commercial premises were financially unviable for a population of such a scale and make no provision for their inclusion, thereby perpetuating the prevailing pattern of car-dependent settlements lacking the critical mass of services needed to become viable communities. For the EDC, however, cultivating a vibrant atmosphere by creating opportunities for residents to interact was integral to the wider ambition, and indicative of its long-term interest in building a rounded, desirable place to live.

Since the arrival of the first residents in February 2015, the EDC has tried to engineer community feeling, organising Christmas celebrations, charity bike rides and even gin tastings. Each new resident gets invited to participate in a tree-planting event and barbeque, in which saplings are planted within a new recreational woodland at the east of the site. Increasingly, though, community spirit is becoming self-engendering. Residents have staged Burns Night Celebrations and organised mother and baby groups. 'The biggest triumph so far has been the

Right /
The Hut in Liddell Park will be Chapelton's community hub, indicative of the EDC's objective to create a vibrant, socially rich town.

social element', says The Duchess of Fife. 'Encouraging the sense of collective ownership is really important to us. Chapelton is only going to be a success if everyone buys into the idea.'[16]

This sentiment drove the establishment of the Chapelton Community Interest Company (CCIC), a not-for-profit entity responsible for the management and maintenance of the town's communal spaces, funded by a flat annual charge to households. All civic facilities, parks, some roads and any other common parts of the town that have not passed into the control of Aberdeenshire Council are owned by CCIC. Any profits are reinvested back into Chapelton. Each homeowner receives one share in the Company so that, although the EDC is currently the principal shareowner, residents will eventually become the collective primary stockholder and assume control of Chapelton's management. The scheme is still in its infancy and its role is arguably still hazy for some inhabitants, yet the goal is to make its denizens active participants in its running. Taking ownership of the town will breed a sense of pride, which in itself will prove a glue that binds the community together.

Whilst the concept is rare within standard UK housing developments, there are several precedents of management companies being used to oversee the delivery and administration of planned settlements. In Letchworth Garden City in Hertfordshire, for example, the Letchworth Heritage Foundation manages the estate, funded by its significant town-centre holdings, and contributes to local activities and charitable objectives; London's Hampstead Garden Suburb is superintended by a trust that proactively maintains the aesthetic qualities of the Suburb; and Poundbury in Dorset has three management companies that are each responsible for the upkeep of its successive phases. No one model is the same as another, but almost all precedents are underpinned by the view that proactive management improves community experience and aesthetics, and that good design is a stimulus to long-term land value. These precepts inform the management vehicle that the EDC framed for Chapelton.

In addition to coordinating common areas and amenities, the CCIC is responsible for upholding the master plan and architectural characteristics of the town as codified in the Design Framework. Aesthetic regulation is a key function of most management bodies. At Poundbury, for instance, requirements are written into homeowner covenants to prevent alterations to exterior wall colour, changes of use, tree removal and any other modifications to the external property; any adjustments must first be approved by the landowner, the Duchy of Cornwall. The rationale behind such prescriptions is simple: it ensures that the integrity of the urban and architectural language of the settlement is maintained over time. For homeowners, it can bring the security that neighbours cannot make adverse alterations that detrimentally affect their own property and its value.

Property covenants are not the norm in the UK and, whilst critics inveigh against their prescriptiveness, a report commissioned by the Rowntree Foundation suggests that,

at Poundbury at least, residents welcome them as a means of enforcing standards:

> Most residents have moved into Poundbury with full knowledge of the restrictions and,
> in some instances, because of the restrictions… Residents felt that the existence of
> covenants provides a structure for disputes between neighbours to be resolved and,
> as a result, reduces potential conflict between neighbours.[17]

Following the Poundbury template, Chapelton uses conditions embedded into
homeowners' legal agreements as a mechanism for design control. Any resident
wishing to make external modifications, whether this be changing paint colours,
replacing a hedge with fencing or exchanging lawn for hardstanding, must first
seek permission from the CCIC review panel, which ensures that any alterations,
regardless of scale, adhere to the aesthetic regulations. To date, this level of
control seems to be recognised as a virtue by homeowners. It may be restrictive
to the individual homeowner, but the security it brings to the long-term value of
their property is appreciated. The EDC also built a further layer of regulation into
Chapelton's structure. As part of the planning permission, Aberdeenshire Council
removed the permitted development rights usually afforded to property owners.
As a result, all exterior changes require formal planning applications to the Council.
Thus, as the town grows and the population evolves, the ethos of Chapelton as
envisioned by the EDC at the outset will be perpetuated.

To date, the EDC remains very much The Duke and Duchess of Fife; they manage
everything, from catering at meetings to chairing public liaison committees to
negotiating land sales with the house builders. Residents have a strong sense of their
involvement from their frequent presence on site and at community events; the EDC

is not a faceless corporation for them. Chapelton is a personal project for the Duke and Duchess, one that they anticipate being involved in for decades to come.

Their zeal for the venture has been pivotal to its success so far. 'They committed themselves unreservedly to becoming experts in all aspects of town building, from the technical to the cultural to the business side', Duany has praised.[18] Even the initial step of commissioning the charrette should not be underestimated. To design the whole scheme was an expensive undertaking at a time when Chapelton had no guaranteed place within the Local Development Plan; the documentation thus generated, though, arguably proved decisive in securing its position within the planning process. 'Chapelton would not be possible without a landowner as committed as The Duke of Fife', John Stephen, managing director of A & J Stephen, has affirmed.[19] The Duke's long-term, vested interest in the site means that, unlike a conventional volume developer, he is prepared to wait for a return on his investment. This, according to Kim Slowe, former managing director of ZeroC, is essential for high-quality, traditional-urbanism schemes like Chapelton that break the mould of standard residential developments in the UK today:

> These types of developments do not achieve the land value premium in the first phase, which is why they are not replicated by national house builders. Over the medium- to long-term, however, the premium to the landowner is significant. We have seen this at Poundbury.[20]

The Duke and Duchess's lifelong interest in the estate gives them a freedom to innovate that standard developers, tied to the need to generate expeditious returns, do not possess. Chapelton is innovative in its nature. Notwithstanding the retrospective cast of its vernacular architecture, its approach is inventive in working with modern regulations and challenging them where this will result in a better place.

Delivering the vision has not been easy. 'Thanks to the amount of support at Scottish Government-level for what Chapelton is aiming to achieve', said landscape architect Janet Benton, 'I thought the main difficulty would be the design and commercial side. In fact, the biggest challenge is simply getting it built.'[21] That the town has come so far and overcome a catalogue of hurdles is testimony to the dedication and enthusiasm of the collective ensemble of legal advisers, architects, landscape designers, house builders, engineers, planning consultants, project managers, contractors and more, working together to fulfil the Chapelton vision. ◆

Right ╱
Like many aspects of Chapelton's urban realm, the road name plates are a 'non-standard detail', specially designed and made for the town.

CHAPTER THREE
DESIGNING THE VISION

Chapelton takes its form from a high-level master plan, the product of a charrette in 2010 (see pages 43–6), authored by the Florida-based, pioneering town-planning practice DPZ, led by Andrés Duany. In the intervening years, this blueprint has been refined. Brooks Murray Architects has given shape to its buildings and Benton Scott-Simmons has imagined its open spaces, conditioned by the architecture, urbanism and landscape of the region.

Under the master plan, 840 hectares of agricultural land is transformed into a nexus of seven neighbourhoods plus a town centre, separated from existing residential settlements in the vicinity by a generous green buffer zone. A hierarchical network of roads and open spaces weaves throughout the plan, providing the structure upon which its urban form hangs and linking each of the neighbourhoods. While the town centre is designed as Chapelton's commercial and civic heart, shops, schools, dentists and other amenities are also distributed throughout the individual neighbourhoods, clustered in their highest proximity at designated neighbourhood centres. Embodying the concept of the pedestrian shed, which Duany calls 'the scale of all urbanism', each centre is positioned to be on average no more than five-or-so-minutes' walk from the neighbourhood edge.[01] Residents' daily needs will thus be accessible within a short stroll from their homes, encouraging the type of walkable, sociable lifestyles that towns and villages of the past seem organically to promote but which the monocultural nature of conventional residential developments of the last half-century inherently preclude. Every neighbourhood contains a mix of housing types — from flats, to terraces, to large farm steadings — to enable a rounded population from the young to the old and a range of environments progressing from the urban to the rural.

The continuum of environments, from urban to rural, higher to lower density, is a sequence that is commonly encountered in the urban fabric of historic towns but it is rarely replicated in modern development in the UK. It is, however, a defining organisational principle of DPZ's approach to master planning. Dubbed transect planning, the design method has been developed by Duany to ensure that the placement, intensity and nature of building is appropriate to a given area. It arranges all elements of the built world – building, plot, street, landscape et al. – into a rural-to-urban progression true to locational character. Rural components are thereby assigned to rural locations, and urban components to urban locations, much as, within the natural world, flora and fauna coexist within the habitats most suited to support them.[02]

The concept of the transect originated, in fact, in the study of biological ecosystems. It was first conceived at the turn of the nineteenth century by Alexander von Humboldt who, in his study of the zonation of plant and animal life in Latin

America, used it to articulate his theory of nature as an intricate web of life, in which every organism has its place within a natural hierarchy. Come the twentieth century, the transect began to be applied in the service of urban thinkers to understand the relationships that shaped cities. In 1909, the Scottish botanist, sociologist, educator and town planner, Patrick Geddes, published his 'Valley Section'. The diagram is a schematic illustration of a regional watershed, tracing the course of a river from its source in the mountains to the open sea, correlating physical conditions with basic occupations in a declension of human livelihoods and settlements. Each type of environment, Geddes was suggesting, organically conditioned a corresponding human economy and each region was in turn shaped by the integration of people into the given qualities of the environment. The Valley Section conceptualised how conditions and contexts differ across a given landscape, thus illustrating the need for sensitivity to antecedents within urban planning.[03]

It was the beginning of a new approach to planning, one that encompassed a full assimilation of the geographical, historical and cultural conditions of a community. Town planning, Geddes wrote, 'is not merely place-planning, nor even work planning. If it is to be successful, it must be folk planning.' The task of town planning, he continued,

> is not to coerce people into new places against their associations, wishes and interest – as we find bad schemes trying to do. Instead its task is to find the right places for each sort of people; places where they will really flourish. To give people in fact the same care that we give when transplanting flowers.[04]

Geddes' efforts to rationalise the interaction between regions and the built environments within them, and to understand a site's existing urban, regional and

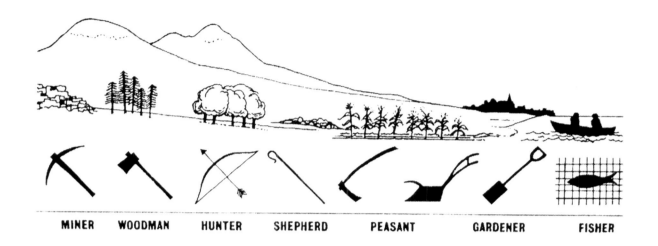

Above /
Patrick Geddes' Valley Section (1909) conceptualised the relationship between human settlements and natural environments. By exploring how conditions change across a landscape, it implies the importance of contextual sensitivity to both natural and urban communities.

ecological conditions, formed the point of origin for Duany's theoretical exploration of the transect. Duany has evolved the transect into a model for understanding the progression of urban form from uninhabited countryside to city core, and thus into a tool for establishing a suitable graduation of intensity within the built environment. 'At the rural end of the continuum', Duany and Emily Talen have set out,

> standards would call for less density; smaller, detached buildings; deep setbacks; paths, trails and open swales; and irregular plantings. At the most urban end of the continuum, standards would call for higher density; larger, attached buildings; shallow setbacks; street and alley sections; and formal plantings. From rural to urban, the density and complexity of human elements are increased, while the density and complexity of natural elements are decreased.[05]

Transect planning is tied to code-based systems, the best known of which is DPZ's Smart Code. The Smart Code divides the rural-to-urban transect into six environments, or zones: rural preserve, rural reserve, sub-urban, general urban, urban centre and urban core. To each of these it applies standards for development, from plot size, to building height, function and signage, to ensure that the constituent components of the zone reinforce its character within the spectrum from rural edge to man-made centre. The Code, its proponents maintain, is flexible; it needs to be to ensure that one transect ecozone flows into the next. However, straying too far from its rules and intermixing rural and urban elements to the extent that it compromises locational identity, is, Duany argues, what leads to sprawl.[06]

It was this transect methodology that DPZ brought to Scotland for the 2010 Chapelton charrette. Its Smart Code, adapted for the Aberdeenshire context, formed

T5 **Urban Centre**
Chapelton's most dense, mixed-use areas operate as urban centres. These include the town centre and some of the neighbourhood centres.

T4 **General Urban**
Chapelton's urban residential neighbourhoods, featuring terrace houses and other relatively dense housing types, can be categorised as general urban.

T3 **Sub-Urban**
Chapelton's quieter residential streets are considered sub-urban, and may include detached houses and houses set on larger plots.

T2 **Rural**
Chapelton's rural edges are developed with low-density farmsteads, designed to preserve the sight lines to the open green space beyond.

CS **Civic Space**
Includes dedicated civic space, such as parks and community areas.

an ordinance framework for the Chapelton master plan. 'I found it a liberating technique', commented Janet Benton, who has been the project's landscape architect since 2010.

> The whole approach to the master plan is driven by an empirical set of structuring principles that has been tried and tested over many years. I have, though, found that people sometimes misinterpreted this systemisation, thinking that because DPZ comes with the same method each time, it delivers the same product each time. But this fails to take into account the way local urban typologies are used for reference, and the sensitivity to the unique qualities of the site, that ensures a responsive, locally appropriate outcome. Each output is different, dependent on the site.[07]

Detailed research went into building a comprehensive, place-specific transect for Chapelton, from a study of the estate's landscape character and that of its surrounding area, to synoptic surveys of the urban patterns and architectural forms of north-east Scotland.

The Chapelton master plan structures the town into a continuous network of transect zones, giving a sense of progression from the rural boundary to the urban centre by subtle but distinct changes in plot size, property set backs, building types and treatment of planting. Within each neighbourhood, there will be a transition from the quieter, outlying blocks of purely residential streets, through increasing densities and greater mix of uses, to the local centre. Already, this rhythm is detectable in the portion of Cairnhill, the first neighbourhood, that has been built. It begins at the approach road, lined by a rustic drystone wall and informal long grass, which leads to the edge of the town and large detached houses. As the route along Greenlaw Road, Cairnhill's main thoroughfare, moves forward, house plots gradually begin to grow smaller, pushing buildings closer to one another, and semi-detached properties appear. When we reach Hume Square, Chapelton's first neighbourhood green, the streetscape increases in density and formality. The lawned square is ringed by a regimented line of ornamental flowering cherry trees. It is defined on three sides by terraces, composed of two-storey houses, flats and Chapelton's first commercial properties – a café, nursery and hair and beauty salon. The shift from one transect zone to the next is discreet but palpable.

Small groupings of shops are strategically inserted, as at Hume Square, into the master plan, building in intensity towards the neighbourhood centre to pepper the town with life. Residents will have the option to pop out for a pint of milk, go to the hairdresser or collect a prescription without getting in their car. Trite as it may sound, it is these types of activities that build a community: they create opportunities for the inhabitants to interact with one another.

All aspects of Cairnhill's streetscapes, from the street widths to the housing details, are conditioned by the transect zones and each of the individual components are subject to overarching design controls. The town is being built to a suite of documents, the Chapelton Design Framework, that guides the architecture, road network, landscape features and infrastructure in accordance with the EDC's vision.

Previous page /
Chapelton's hierarchical transect plan.

Design codes are a tool used frequently within New Urbanism and traditional urbanism to uphold the principles of the transect in the context of the master plan, but, as related in the first chapter, such guidelines have historically been used within new settlement creation in Scotland for centuries to ensure architectural harmony and building standards. The Chapelton Design Framework essentially provides a recipe book for the physical character of Cairnhill. Block by block, street by street, the Framework sets out house types, materials, street design, landscape character and planting, providing both explicit guidelines for contractors to work to and a sense of certainty to the local authority of the form that Chapelton will take. It integrates the entire design process across professional disciplines, within the rural-to-urban spectrum of the master plan.

The landscape and street networks are the structural lynchpins upon which the master plan hangs. The emphasis upon the former is one of the key distinguishing factors of Chapelton when pitted against conventional volume developments. 'All too often, open spaces tend to be the leftover bits', according to Benton. 'The commercial aspect means that the most attractive and level parts of the site are used for housing, and the surplus, more challenging, land is used as the green space element.' At Chapelton, pockets of open space are continuously interwoven into the master plan. It is a costly approach, in terms of both implementation and maintenance, but it reflects the commitment to creating pedestrian-friendly, visually stimulating neighbourhoods. Chapelton's plan illustrates a connected matrix of green corridors, used to define and link the areas of the settlement, interrupted at regular intervals by 'events' – small parks, squares and so forth. Cyclists thus have a fluid network to move across the town, and children have safe, comfortable routes to walk to school.

Landscape corridors run east to west across the site, interconnecting with small, secondary north-to-south channels to form a finely grained structure. The most substantial of the east-to-west links runs along the Burn of Elsick, one of several watercourses on the estate that was used in the early planning stages to give shape to the town's design. The plan is highly responsive to the existing landscape features of the site. This is indicative of the hand of Duany, whose contextual approach to master planning seeks to use the 'traces of the land' – a phrase he borrows from early-twentieth-century town planner Raymond Unwin – as underpinning components of any design.[8] Blocks of existing woodland, drystone walls, field patterns, farm tracks and agricultural drainage channels were integrated into the plan to help preserve as much of the extant character of the landscape as practicable and ensure that Chapelton is a town rooted in its locality. The alignment of Bunting Place, for example, extending at an angle north west from Hume Square (plate XXIX), mimics an old field boundary. 'One of the great pleasures of Andrés's team and the way they work', The Duke of Fife has reflected,

> is that the urban planning very much followed the traces on the land, whether man made or natural. Every effort was made to keep the character of the place, to keep all the existing buildings and features as far as we could. To me, it was a comfort to think that the place where I had grown up was going to be respected and reflected in the town plan.[09]

Where it has not been possible to retain features, their 'traces' are often still visible. Wherever feasible, the footprint of the large stretches of existing coniferous stands – themselves of limited amenity or ecological value because of their monocultural uniformity – are preserved in the plan and will gradually be replanted with mixed native species. Meanwhile, many of the drystone walls cannot be preserved intact due to the frangible nature of their construction, but their material is saved and employed elsewhere. Similarly, large boulders excavated from the rocky site have been reused at the town entrance (plate III) or to mark plot boundaries. It is such thoughtful details that are helping to create an identity for the town.

In line with the transect zoning of the master plan, features like boulders and drystone walls occur with greater frequency towards the rural margins than in the urban core of the town. There is a subtle but definite change in the formality of open spaces, the plant species used and how they are maintained as one moves through this continuum. Greenlaw Road, for instance, has large avenue trees planted in grass verges and garden boundaries strongly delineated with formal hedging, drystone walls or fencing to reflect its significance as the arrival route into Cairnhill; whereas in Nether Cairnhill Lane, a tertiary neighbourhood thoroughfare at the edge of the town, trees are more loosely, more softly arranged and only one side of the carriageway has a footway. Similarly, Hume Square in the 'general urban' transect zone is a much more formal environment than Pheppie Park (plate XXII) at the south-east fringe of the town, categorised as 'sub-urban'; compare the rigid geometry and lines of trees of the former to the relaxed conformation of the latter, with meadow planting around its perimeter.

The structuring principles of the transect framework guide the distribution of the open spaces, from the 13.5-hectare town park at the urban core to the 33.5-hectare community woodland at the east of the site (see page 52). Chapelton has a full complement of landscapes, just as would be found in historic Scottish settlements. Some 200 hectares have been allocated to open space, ranging from a country park, to neighbourhood greens, sports pitches, allotments and agricultural plots on the town's southern and eastern fringes. Each one is designed to be legible, distinguishable in form and purpose. Pheppie Park, for example, is a secluded local garden tucked amongst houses and ringed by ornamental trees and long grass. Children, Benton hopes, will play ball games on its central lawn; the fencing of the surrounding houses is kept deliberately low so the park is well overlooked to provide a safe place for them, even if unaccompanied. Burgess Park, in contrast, has a more public, formal character. Bounded to its east by Black Street and on its remaining sides by ten terraced properties, it will be a small lawned square defined on the roadside by metal railings and a row of trees. Few standard volume developments strive towards this variety in landscape provision; it simply does not add up commercially.

Variety is no less discernable in the road network, which functions in tandem with the open space matrix to give form to the town plan. Chapelton is an intricate web of street types, based upon a hierarchy of function. Main thoroughfares, such as

Above ╱
Murray Street, a secondary
thoroughfare within
Chapelton's road hierarchy.

Greenlaw Road, form the overall block structure and connect the neighbourhood centres; secondary and tertiary thoroughfares provide access to and run between residential blocks; lanes are shared between foot and vehicular traffic to access parking and garages at the rear of plots; and narrow pedestrian-only passageways intersect blocks to provide cut-throughs for foot traffic. Roads become wider with more parking provisions the more traffic they are intended to carry and the greater mix of uses and users they accommodate. This type of gradated diversity is common to traditional Scottish settlements; it partly answers for why they make for such visually edifying places to move through.

The entire Chapelton street network is designed to be coherent and legible for pedestrians, cyclists and motorists. Much of this legibility is down to the fact that its lines are based on precedents. Several of the main thoroughfares follow existing minor roads and tracks that link the scattered farms and residences on the estate and near vicinity; each block is designed to hew to the contours of the land. The typology of the streets, furthermore, is closely linked to praxis in Scottish towns and villages. Like the approach to landscape, this belongs to an overarching ambition to tie the fledgling town to its locality. Inspired by Patrick Geddes' 'city surveys', the design team analysed the urban ingredients and proportions of the most admired cities, towns and villages in Aberdeenshire and beyond to discover the constitutive vernacular of the environment of the North East. The carriageway widths, kerb types, average plots sizes, building set backs and so forth of places including Aberdeen, Montrose and Stonehaven were documented to reveal the pattern language of the region, which then informed the master plan. Hume Square, for instance, is loosely based on an antecedent in the Aberdeenshire village of Monymusk.

The master plan, though, is less reflective of direct parallels and more interested in capturing a regional parlance. Note the pend on the north side of Hume Square, providing glimpses into a courtyard beyond (Plate XXXII); or North Bell Rock Lane (plate XVI), cutting through the block to provide access to garages and parking provisions in the manner of traditional wynds; or Painter Close (plate XVII), a narrow pedestrian passageway linking Nether Cairnhill Drive to a service lane behind, of the type that can be found in great numbers in Montrose, St Andrews and elsewhere. This variety of traditional street types within the block pattern makes travelling through Cairnhill simultaneously a more interesting and an easier experience. Whether on foot or in a vehicle, the blocks are permeable and well-connected, avoiding the bottlenecks that are often associated with modern cul-de-sac development. The streets' design makes clear distinction where traffic is dominant and where, as in the back lanes and closes, pedestrians and cyclists have priority. Whereas Greenlaw Road, a main thoroughfare, for example, has an upstand kerb and change in surface material to signal the difference between the road and footpath, Nether Cairnhill Lane is designed as a shared space for cars and pedestrians. At a maximum of seven metres wide, the single-lane wynd has no conventional carriageway-footway separation.

Chapelton's approach to motor vehicles is refreshing. The town is planned to accommodate the car. Within twenty-first-century life, it is quixotic to attempt otherwise. Yet, it is not designed *for* the car; it is designed primarily for people. There is a distinct lack of white lines and traffic signs; vehicles are controlled not by humps or road signage, but calmed using irregular angles, tree planting or changes in surfaces. At the opening of North Bell Rock Lane, for instance, a band of granite setts signals the transition in traffic regime from the secondary thoroughfare Black Street into the shared-space lane; within the lane, a bird cherry tree planted at the edge but within the carriageway creates a natural obstacle around which cars must manoeuvre (plate XLIII).

North Bell Rock Lane is one of Cairnhill's many back lanes, housing garages and dedicated parking accessible from the rear of properties. Parking in Cairnhill is, almost universally, distributed in rear courtyards and on the street. 'One of our biggest successes at Chapelton', champions Benton, 'is that we have displaced cars from front gardens. It is a major achievement in terms of the character of the streetscape.' Chapelton runs counter to the pattern of most modern residential developments by removing driveways from the plot fronts to achieve enclosed gardens. 'We wondered how residents would adapt to having to go to the rear of their house to get their car', Benton continued, 'but this hasn't been an issue, probably because it is not, in fact, an unfamiliar situation. After all, if you buy a traditional town house or flat in city-centre Aberdeen, the arrangement would be the same.'[10] This layout permits several advantages. Inserting parking at the front of plots is a land-hungry approach; it immediately has the effect of pushing the buildings apart and broadening the width of the street. Dislodging parking to the rear enables more efficient use of land. Furthermore, without a barricade of cars before each house, streetscapes are immediately improved; they not only look more harmonious but, with narrower plots, neighbours are also brought within talking distance. Several of Cairnhill's residential streets are totally car free. The terrace-lined Bunting Place or Rennie Place with its detached houses are such examples, inspired by pedestrian thoroughfares like Wrights' and Coopers' Place in Old Aberdeen.

The influence of local building patterns is felt not only in Chapelton's urban character, but also in its housing. Architecture is designed to reflect the context of northern Scotland. Externally, buildings are predominantly clad in render and roofed in natural grey slate, materials that are frequently used within the Aberdeenshire vernacular and so compatible with the North East's climate. The palette is kept deliberately narrow, for both cost reasons and to bring cohesion and thus identity to the wider ensemble. It is, however, enlivened, particularly within the blocks, by flashes of colour or changing textures – red clay pantile roofs, timber garages, brightly painted doors. Variety is thereby achieved with few variables. Buildings employ the simple silhouettes that characterise traditional houses in Scottish villages and towns, but they are animated by playful eaves, roof lines interrupted by dormers, pitched-roof porches and knotted timber columns (plate VII).

The types of houses within Chapelton were also inspired by Scottish precedents. Timber-clad cottages in Cromarty, mews houses in Footdee, shops with living space above in Aberdeen, terraces in Dunkeld and a cottage in Findhorn (plate VIII) are all invoked in Chapelton's architecture. Cairnhill's first phase, the initial 802 homes, is planned to contain 69 different house types, from flats in Hume Square (plate XXIX), to terraces in Bunting Place (plate XXVIII), cottages in Farquharson Street (plate XXXIX), semi-detached houses in Murray Street (plate XXXV), detached dwellings in Nether Cairnhill Drive (plate XIII) and large farmsteads on the town edge. Their distribution is, again, determined by the transect: the further from the core, the bigger the property and the lower the density. In the short term, this diversity will, it is hoped, draw a varied mix of inhabitants to Chapelton of differing family sizes, incomes and housing preferences; and in the long term, it will enable them to stay in the town as they downsize in retirement or upscale as their families grow. Visually, the diversity also vitalises the streetscapes.

Only a small portion of Chapelton has yet been realised, but already the urban experience is a multifaceted one. It is a pleasurable place through which to move. Streets gently curve, drawing our eyes onwards; groupings of trees or a lawned green make for focal points or interruptions; grass verges move inwards and outwards to frame the road. Increasingly, as more of the town is completed, a walk through Chapelton will be a progression of subtly varying sequences; around each bend, or at the top of each slope will be a new street vignette. Raymond Unwin, the early-twentieth-century planner who has had such an influence on Duany's approach to master planning, called these 'street pictures'. Derived from the writings of nineteenth-century Austrian urbanist Camillo Sitte, the concept involved thinking of the built environment as a series of vistas, and we see it in Unwin's work at Letchworth Garden City and Hampstead Garden Suburb.

Left /
Flashes of colour and changing
roof lines enliven Chapelton's
street scenes.

Its legacy is also at play in Chapelton. The variation in road widths, the lanes and pedestrian closes that cut through blocks, the pockets of green or breaks in the street line have the effect of creating sequential street scenes that allow the pedestrian, or cyclist, or motorist, to engage with their surroundings. This will only heighten as hedges grow and trees mature. There is no sense of sameness in Chapelton, no prolonged rows of identical houses; but neither is there variety for variety's sake. Each streetscape is treated individually, done so within the regulating maxims of the transect and Design Framework and reflective of the topography of the land. In Nether Cairnhill Drive (plate XII), for instance, the houses use the same vernacular language, their materials are taken from the same restricted palette, and yet through the alternation in roof lines, the set backs of houses, the projection of porches and the sweeping bend of the road as it descends the natural gradient, the whole coalesces into an urban ensemble that is visually and viscerally stimulating.

The importance of injecting artistic experience into the residents' day-to-day life should not be underestimated. Whether on a conscious or subliminal level, the built environment weaves a spell on our psyche, behaviour and wellbeing.[11] Architecture, wrote John Ruskin, 'is the art which so disposes and adorns the edifices raised by man, for whatsoever uses, that the sight of them may contribute to his mental health, power, and pleasure'.[12] The quietly imaginative treatment that characterises the design of Chapelton's urban realm creates an aesthetically rewarding experience for its residents.

More often than not, though, discussions about Chapelton's design focus not upon the holistic urban experience but upon architectural style. Its adherence to traditional morphologies has been polemic. The strong aversion many design professionals aver towards locationally and historically referenced architecture means they find it impossible to divorce the wider urban, sustainability and community objectives of the settlement from its clothing. The wider public, conversely, evinces a general enthusiasm for this style.[13] There is certainly an economic case to be made for traditional architecture. Between 1983 and 2013, terraced houses in London that were built prior to World War I increased in value by 465 per cent compared to 255 per cent for post-war terraces.[14] Meanwhile, a study of new-build house sales in the Netherlands published in 2017 concluded that, even controlling for a wide range of factors, there is a price premium of 15 per cent for pure neo-traditional styles over non-traditional houses.[15]

It is not anticipated that the architectural mode used for the initial phase of Cairnhill will continue across the whole of Chapelton. The commitment to investing in high-quality architecture will remain, but diversification is part of the natural growth of any town. Likewise, the master plan is not ironclad. Following the 2010 charrette, Brooks Murray Architects tweaked and tuned the DPZ blueprint to better suit the road network to the contours of the land. More recently, it has revised aspects in conjunction with the three house builders to reflect the changing market. On Farquharson Street, for instance, eight planned detached houses were replaced by 20 two-bedroom cottages arranged akin to almshouses in three courts. Pragmatically, this change reflects the drop in demand for large properties following the slump in Aberdeen's oil industry.

Flexibility, the whole team has learnt, needs to be built into the master planning outlook. Versatility is an especial priority for the landscape design, according to Benton:

> A lesson I've grasped at Chapelton is that we cannot predict exactly who or what we are designing for, we do not know who the residents will be or to what use they will put the open spaces. So we try to keep the green spaces simple and flexible, accepting that others will make their imprint on those spaces and that their use and appearance will evolve.[16]

The planting, too, will evolve with time. Like the architecture, the same approach will not be employed across the whole site. There is also an element of experimentation. Approximately 32 hectares of new planting is proposed, including over 5,000 trees in parks, civic spaces, avenues, car parks and gardens, distributed in adherence with the transect zoning. Planned species, the majority of which are native, include beech, hornbeam, oak, rowan, elder, pine and cherry. The site, though, presents technical challenges for planting. The land's close proximity to the coast means it can be subject to haar and salt-laden sea winds. Its underlying geography, furthermore, is rugged. Rock lies close to the surface in places resulting in shallow soil.

The topography is also a challenge for the master planners and architects. 'Scottish geology is the most difficult we have experienced', said Duany of the master-planning process. The granite beneath the surface, he explained, meant 'virtually every road needed to be nudged into a more sensitive alignment with the geological condition'.[17] Chapelton is an undulating site. On the one hand, this lends itself to picturesque layouts; on the other, it means gradients must be frequently negotiated (plate XLVIII). House plots on Greenlaw Road, for example, are built up behind drystone walls. Cairnhill's traditional Scottish street types, such as wynds, are in themselves some of the best means of addressing the hilly site, providing links within blocks to streets of different heights, for example.

The design team have also faced man-made challenges. 'It has proven much harder than originally anticipated to replicate traditional urban typologies', says Benton. 'Modern standards, particularly road standards, means that it is very difficult to build the diversity and character of old towns.' The lanes, for instance, are wider than first intentioned in accordance with current stipulations, and pavements are bigger than those of historic precedents that the design team looked at. '"Standards" result in everything increasing in scale, pushing built elements apart, increasing street dimensions and losing a sense of intimacy', Benton continued. 'It makes the charm of traditional villages and towns very difficult to recreate now. By definition, "standards" imply keeping variations to a minimum, so any deviation, even something simple such as the use of granite setts, requires considerable time and effort to gain approval.'[18] The very fact that granite setts do feature within Chapelton is a reflection of the long-term thinking of the EDC. Securing approval for these and other elements from the relevant statutory authorities is a lengthy, costly exercise that many conventional

builders would not attempt because of their transient interest in the site. The Duke and Duchess of Fife's longstanding concern in Chapelton, however, has underpinned much of the decision-making within the design process. This is reflected in the attitude towards planting, for they are content that plants take years to become established, or in the hand-crafted drystone wall that lines the approach roach to Chapelton. The latter was a big expenditure, entailing specialist artisans, but it has become one of the most lauded aspects of the built environment: it immediately establishes an identity for the young town. The long-term vision of the EDC has inspired a similar commitment within the design team. 'As a consultant, it is rare to work on a project for this length of time', says Benton. 'Being able to see Chapelton grow and to learn from it is a privilege that does not happen often.'[19]

Chapelton is a living, growing entity. Its built setting and open spaces are evolving as the town grows and lessons are appropriated. Three central principles, though, have defined its design from the outset. The most important of these is arguably the transect, organising the various elements of the environment in a rural-to-urban continuum that is true to locational character. The second is the use of regional architectural, urbanism and planting precedents to give this very new place roots in its locality, an immediate identity and the types of spaces that have proven themselves successful over generations. From their study of historic villages, towns and cities, the design team learnt the value of variety, the third principle. Through subtle and contextual variation, streetscapes are given life. Chapelton is yet only a fraction of what it will be in decades to come, yet through the application of these tenets, it already has the essence of a true town, not a monochromatic housing estate, but a diverse, pedestrian-orientated place where each phase of life can be played out. ◆

EPILOGUE
CHALLENGING CONVENTIONS

Chapelton is a town in the making. It is still early days in its story, but in the decade since the Elsick Development Company (EDC) was established to promote the idea, enormous progress has been made. The scheme went from having no status in the local planning process in early 2010, to the first homes being occupied in February 2015. It was extremely fortuitous that Aberdeenshire Council had a planning process in place, which created a strong current for the project; but impulsion was also engineered by The Duke and Duchess of Fife. They took a daring and perspicacious step in commissioning the charrette in September 2010, and in deliberately pushing their vision forward.

The journey has been far from smooth. Chapelton's progress has been checked by Aberdeen's housing market downturn, by the logistical challenges of the terrain and by the planning, highways and building regulatory systems. However, enough of the town has been completed to enable the onlooker to appreciate the conviction that has driven the Duke and Duchess from the start: that we can make a better job of developing our towns and cities than is currently being done.

Chapelton is aspiring to a set of objectives that renders it substantially different to twenty-first-century norms. A clear differentiator is its scale. The town is bringing together the area's housing need for the next 40 years onto a single site. It is a radically different approach to the sprawling, piecemeal extensions to existing towns and villages that have defined growth in north-east Scotland in past decades. The very length of the project is indicative of the second differentiator: the long-term presence of the landowner. The Elsick estate has belonged to the Duke's family for six centuries; his interest in the land is deep-rooted. This long-termism gives the EDC the latitude to innovate that a conventional volume developer, answerable to shareholders seeking short-term yields, does not have. From a physical perspective, Chapelton is pursuing an urban model that is familiar within historic Scottish towns, cities and villages but that has been largely lost since the post-war era. Its carefully considered master plan prioritises variety in the street scene, a mix of house types, the inclusion of shops and workplaces, a hierarchical road network and a conscious balancing of the demands of the motor car and the pedestrian. Furthermore, these principles are all being enacted to extremely high standards of design and construction. From a social perspective, the EDC wants to make Chapelton a true community. It is realising this not only through the urban realm's walkability and mixed uses, but also by investing time and care into cultivating bonds between residents and their connection to the town. Following this route adds time, cost and complexity compared to the single-use, suburban product of standard modern developments, but it delivers the third differentiator: a high-quality, human environment.

Achieving these objectives within the current regulatory system is enormously challenging. The planning, road and building regulations that were originally coined to raise the standards of new development now impose such limitations that they can have the opposite outcome. Whilst there has been no shortage of theoretical support at local and national government level for the innovations to which Chapelton aspires, the rigidity of these ordinances has made the town much harder to deliver.

We return to the point made at the opening of the introduction, that the building of new towns is a prodigiously infrequent feat because of the level of complexity involved. Chapelton is a rare and special undertaking. Its materialisation has only been possible thanks to the long-term dedication, fidelity and perseverance of the landowners and all those involved in the project. Chapelton is not perfect; compromises have been made along the way and more will no doubt be made yet. Neither was it ever intended to be a planned utopia; throughout, a watchful eye has been kept on its commercial viability. However, by challenging the conventions of contemporary development, it is breaking new ground in Scotland. It represents optimism and aspiration as we search for lasting solutions to address the increasingly acute urban problems of twenty-first-century society. Perhaps it is apt to give the last word to Ebenezer Howard, that pioneer of urban reform at the turn of the twentieth century:

> One should never be excessively realistic in humane plans. There are always too many difficulties and only a small percentage of aims may be attained. Our aspirations therefore should always be as far-reaching as they can be... And the percentage of losses depends only on the enthusiasm, energy and perseverance of the idealists who undertake it.[01] ◆

PLATES

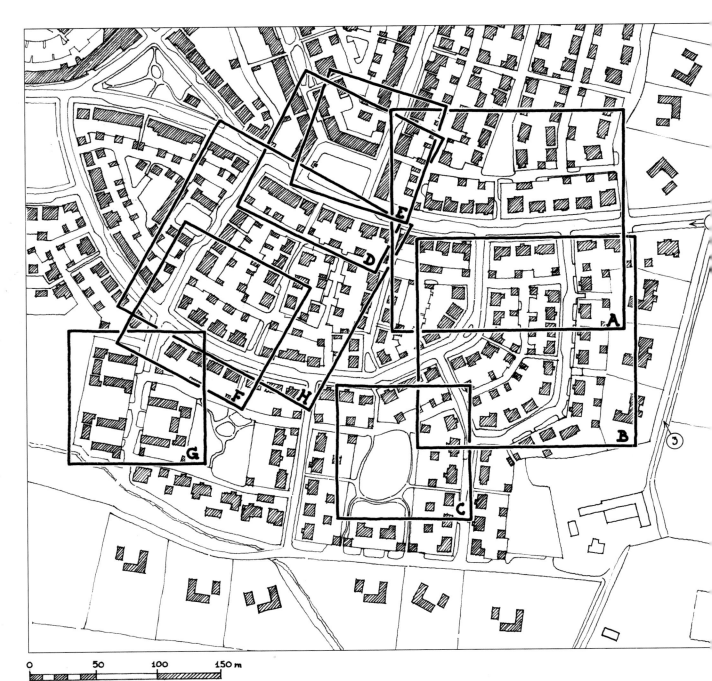

DIAGRAM PLAN OF CAIRNHILL, SOUTH-EAST AREA

The following collection of plans and photographs showcases the development of the town to date. The plans illustrate in detail the eight sections outlined in the above plan marked A to H. In this and the subsequent plans, the numbered arrows correspond to the numbers of the photographs which follow and the direction in which the views have been taken.

1. GREENLAW ROAD

Chapelton's approach road is bounded by a drystone wall, which
physically separates a pedestrian and cycle route from the carriageway.
The wall, made from reclaimed stone from the site, echoes those found in
the surrounding countryside. Its rural character is reflective of its location
at the outermost edge of the town.

2. GREENLAW ROAD

Entrance to the town. When large granite boulders are unearthed on
site, they are saved and reused for end posts for garden boundaries,
informal seats or special features such as this town sign.

3. CAUSEY MOUNTH

View from the Causey Mounth, an ancient drove road that traverses the
eastern part of the site. It belongs to the pre-existing network of roads and
tracks that are retained within the master plan.

SCALE OF METRES

SECTION A

This plan shows in detail the section marked as A in the Diagram Plan.
In this and the subsequent plans, buildings which feature in the following
photographs are hatched, whilst unbuilt areas of the town are shaded grey.

1. GREENLAW ROAD

View west along Greenlaw Road. Grass verges are planted with birch that
will mature into an informal avenue of trees stretching along the full
length of the main arrival route into Chapelton.

2. GREENLAW ROAD

Chapelton reflects regional architectural motifs, such as timber porches
and knotted pine columns, common features in north-east Scotland.

3. GREENLAW ROAD

View east along Greenlaw Road. Its function as Chapelton's approach road is reflected within the public realm and boundary treatments: drystone walls and formal hedges provide definite garden edges whilst grass verges create a clear street edge and separate foot and vehicular traffic.

4. SOUTH ROTHESAY LANE

View into a parking court for houses on Greenlaw Road. Wherever possible, parking in Chapelton is distributed away from the main streets at the rear of properties to allow for more traditional streetscapes. The tree and shrub planting will mature to add colour and texture to the simple hard-surfaced court.

5. MURDOCH LANE

Parking courts from a distance. Where sites for future housing at the
edge of the development have been taken out of agricultural use, they are
seeded to create wildflower grass meadows.

SCALE OF METRES

SECTION B

At the edge of the town. Nether Cairnhill Drive and Murray Street flank a
back lane, Nether Cairnhill Lane, where the parking and garages for the
two thoroughfares are located.

1. NETHER CAIRNHILL DRIVE

The curving road, movement in building lines and variation in
colours give variety to the street scene with few variables.

2. NETHER CAIRNHILL DRIVE

Streets on the outer edge of the development are more rural in character. Nether Cairnhill Drive has a footway on only one side of the carriageway, garden boundaries defined by beech hedging to create a continuous green edge and porches and outbuildings are clad in vertical board-and-batten timber.

3. NETHER CAIRNHILL DRIVE
Nether Cairnhill Drive features some of the larger properties in Chapelton,
reflective of its location at the outskirts of the town.

NETHER CAIRNHILL LANE

4. NORTH BELL ROCK LANE/NETHER CAIRNHILL LANE
Bands of granite setts break up the expanses of hardstanding
within the back lanes.

5. NORTH BELL ROCK LANE

The terminated vista at the end of this back lane provides visual interest
and also adds a degree of surveillance to make the lane feel less secluded
and hence safer.

6. PAINTER CLOSE

View along Painter Close. Closes provide shortcuts through blocks to
increase their permeability. The granite setts indicate the transition into
the close and its pedestrian-only realm.

7. NETHER CAIRNHILL LANE

View of back lane parking garages. Parking places are tucked between garages to render cars less visible, while the combination of colours and materials adds richness to the streetscape.

8. NETHER CAIRNHILL LANE

View into a back lane. Despite an absence of road markings, traffic is passively calmed through the non-uniform geometry of the carriageway and planting beds, which provide small irregularities and localised narrowings.

9. MURRAY STREET

View north-east along Murray Street. The island and cluster of trees in the
centre of the road passively slows traffic.

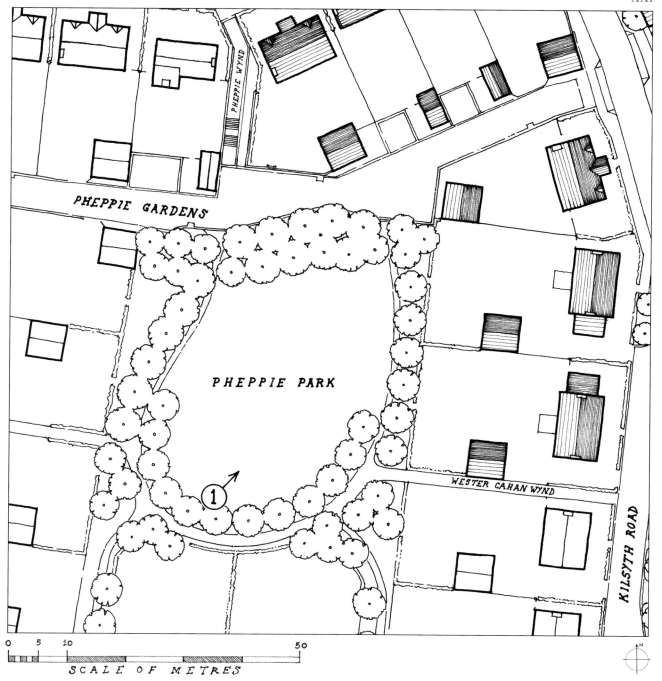

SECTION C

Pheppie Park, an intimate, informal neighbourhood park.

1. PHEPPIE PARK

View of Pheppie Park. Residents in surrounding houses have direct access
from their gardens. Garden boundaries are kept low to provide sightlines
into the park.

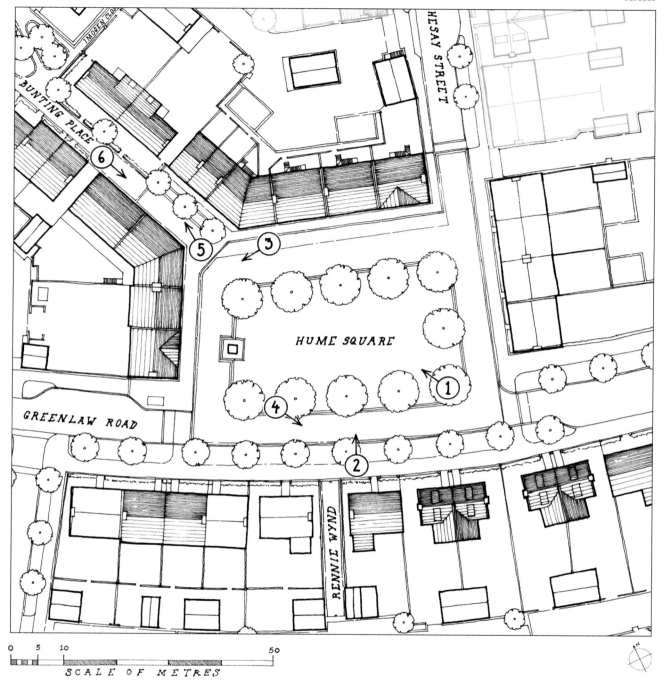

SECTION D

Hume Square, located in the south-east of the Cairnhill neighbourhood and
inspired by the proportions of traditional Aberdeenshire village greens.

1. HUME SQUARE

Hume Square is Chapelton's first 'destination space', a village green
focused upon a formal lawn ringed by regimented ornamental flowering
cherry trees, which, when mature, will create a continuous canopy of
white blossom in spring.

2. HUME SQUARE

View of the north range of Hume Square. Two-storey terraced buildings make for an intimate, human scale. Note the pend, providing access to the parking court behind.

3. HUME SQUARE
Hume Square's combination of shops, houses and flats is indicative of the
master plan's mixed-use approach.

4. HUME SQUARE

South side of Hume Square, named after the revolutionary philosopher David Hume. Chapelton's street names commemorate those who have played a formative role in Scottish history, as well as individuals who have contributed to the town's creation and local places.

5. BUNTING PLACE

Bunting Place is a pedestrian-only thoroughfare lined with a mix of
terraced and semi-detached houses; cars are displaced to parking courts
and lanes behind. An avenue of ornamental flowering cherry trees lines
its centre, extending the tree canopy from Hume Square.

6. BUNTING PLACE

View along Bunting Place to Hume Square beyond. Bunting Place's
alignment correlates with that of an old field boundary. Wherever possible,
the master plan aspires to retain the inherent character of the site.

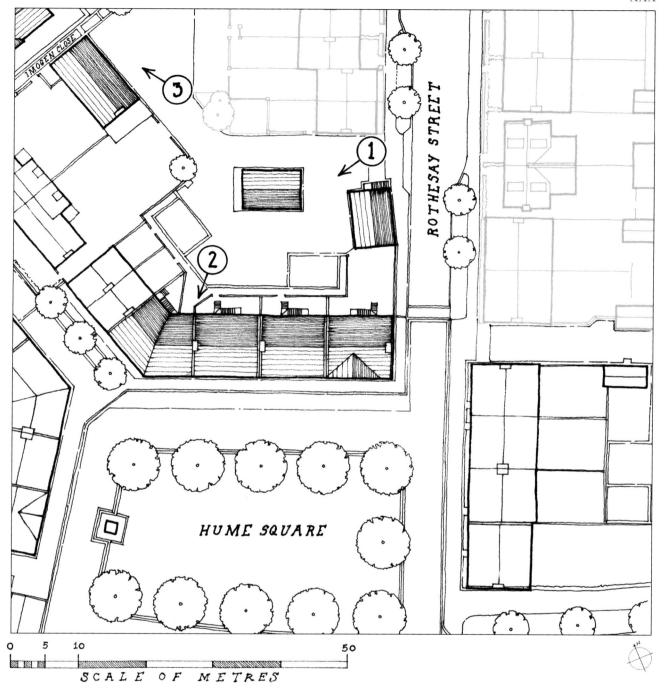

SECTION E

Court behind Hume Square, providing access to Hume Square flats,
timber-clad parking garages and an office unit above a garage. The garages
are important architectural elements in their own right, 'hiding' private
car parking from the main streets. Office space is interwoven amongst
residential uses to create livelier streets, with people coming and going
at different times of the day.

1. ASHLEY LANE

View into the parking court behind Hume Square. The granite setts in the foreground indicate the change in regime from a thoroughfare where vehicles are dominant to a shared-surface lane, where foot and bicycle traffic have priority. Stairs to the office unit are seen on left.

2. ASHLEY LANE

The parking court is linked to Hume Square via a pend, a traditional
Scottish street typology used within the Chapelton master plan to increase
pedestrian connections through the blocks. This design approach can
provide visual stimulation to pedestrians in the form of intriguing views.

3. ASHLEY LANE
A modern interpretation of traditional coach houses, the foreground
shows a flat above parking garages. To its right sits an apartment block,
the main frontage of which faces Bunting Place.

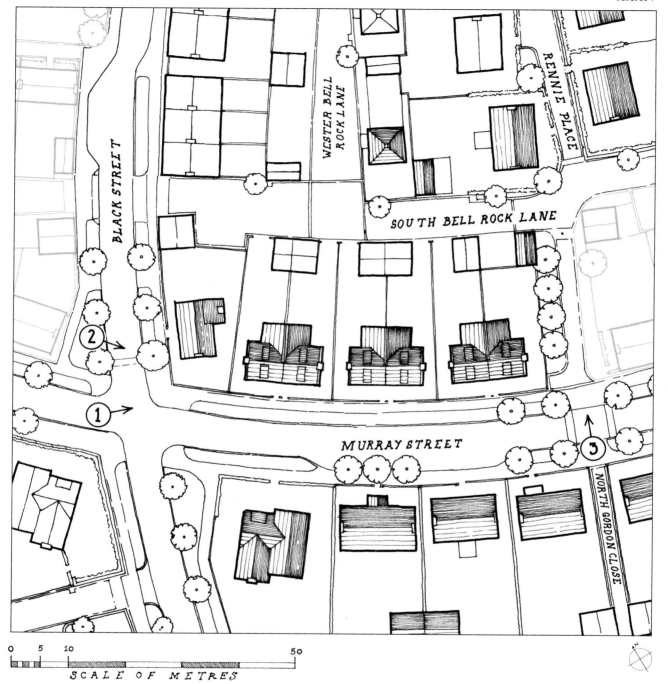

WESTER BELL ROCK LANE

BLACK STREET

RENNIE PLACE

SOUTH BELL ROCK LANE

② →

① →

MURRAY STREET

↑ ③

NORTH GORDON CLOSE

0 5 10 50

SCALE OF METRES

SECTION F

Plan of two secondary thoroughfares, Murray Street and Black Street,
and shared surface lanes providing access to the rear of plots.

1. MURRAY STREET

A single plant species – beech – is used to define garden boundaries.
Once mature, it will form a consistent bold green element in the streetscape.

2. BLACK STREET

These slate-roofed, rendered houses exemplify Chapelton's building palette. The materials are traditional to north-east Scotland. Using a consistent material palette will help to ensure Chapelton develops as a cohesive whole.

3. MURRAY STREET

View northwards along a pedestrian-only road. Chapelton's streets follow
traditional block patterns, which allow for maximum connectivity and
travel across the town via multiple routes.

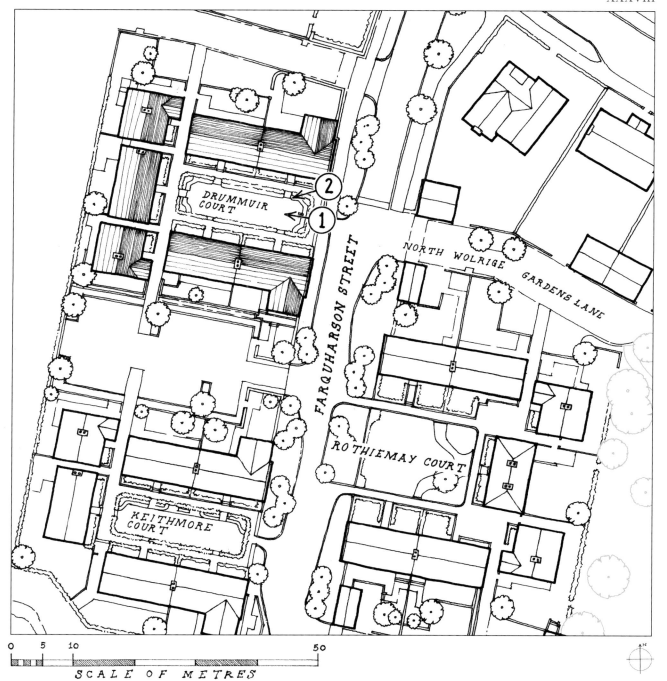

SCALE OF METRES

SECTION G

Twenty single-storey cottages arranged around three courtyards.

1. DRUMMUIR COURT

The courtyard-form echoes historic almshouse morphologies. The central lawns provide sheltered spaces with south-facing benches to create welcoming landscapes.

2. DRUMMUIR COURT

The cottages were added to the master plan in response to housing market demands, illustrative of the plan's and the developers' flexibility to react to changing conditions.

SECTION H

Network of back lanes and pedestrian closes that provides connections
within Chapelton's blocks.

1. BLACK STREET

View east towards Black Street. Terrace housing of different sizes
is grouped within a single street picture.

2. NORTH BELL ROCK LANE

View east along North Bell Rock Lane. The simple back lane housing
garages and parking places is enlivened by the play in roofs, materials
and colours.

3. NORTH BELL ROCK LANE/EASTER BELL ROCK LANE

Junction of Easter Bell Rock Lane and North Bell Rock Lane, a roadway housing parking for properties on Greenlaw Road. Houses overlook Chapelton's back lanes, as seen here, to activate the spaces and provide a sense of security to ensure they are widely used, and are not solely for parking.

4. EASTER BELL ROCK LANE

View to Easter Bell Rock Lane. One of the defining aspects of Chapelton's public realm is its lack of road signs and white lines. Traffic is controlled passively and intuitively using bands of granite setts, tree planting and road geometry.

5. EASTER BELL ROCK LANE
Mews units with off-street parking within a shared-space lane.

6. EASTER BELL ROCK LANE

Beech hedges enclose front gardens. When matured, they will add
greenery to the street scene.

7. RENNIE PLACE

View northwards on Rennie Place. Houses are strategically placed on this pedestrian-only street to minimise long windy corridors and create visual interest through deflected vistas and alternation in building lines.

8. RENNIE PLACE

View northwards on Rennie Place. Boundary treatments are a key element in the streetscape. Here, gardens are defined by drystone walls and beech hedges, both common features within the Aberdeenshire landscape. The latter has the advantage of retaining copper-coloured foliage during the winter.

9. RENNIE PLACE

As seen in Rennie Place, Chapelton makes regular use of materials native
to the region, such as harling, drystone walls and granite.

10. WESTER BELL ROCK LANE
A playful use of colours, materials and rooflines injects subtle variation
into the street scenes.

PROJECT TEAM

A & J STEPHEN
House Builder

AJC HOMES
House Builder

**BENTON
SCOTT-SIMMONS**
Landscape Architects

**BROOKS MURRAY
ARCHITECTS**
Town Architects

BURNESS PAULL
Legal Advisers

DPZ
Master Planners

FAIRHURST
Civil Engineers

**BRIO
RETIREMENT LIVING**
Retirement Community Developer

RSP
Mechanical and
Electrical Engineers

THOMSON GRAY
Cost Consultants

TURNBERRY
Development Strategy and
Planning Consultants

TURNER & TOWNSEND
Project Managers

W. M. DONALD
Infrastructure Contractors

WSP
Road Engineers

ZEROC
House Developer

GLOSSARY

Burgage: A form of tenure by which land lying within royal burghs was held under the crown, the proprietors being liable to nominal services of watching and warding.

Burgage plot: The property owned by a burgess in a medieval town. Burgage plots are characteristically long and narrow, with a row of outbuildings stretching to the rear of the house and shop.

Burgh: A town possessing special privileges conferred by charter and having a municipal corporation.

Burn: A brook or stream.

Close: A narrow pedestrian passageway that traverses a block with housing units and/or commercial uses on each side.

Drystone wall, or drystane dyke: A stone wall constructed without any mortar, and frequently seen in Scotland and Ireland. Dykes are often used to delineate property boundaries or as retaining walls for terraced land.

Enlightenment: European intellectual and philosophical movement of the late seventeenth and eighteenth centuries marked by a rejection of traditional social, religious and political ideas and an emphasis on rationalism.

Fermtoun: A cluster of cottages for the tenants and labourers of a farm.

Feu: The tenure of land in perpetuity in return for a continuing annual payment of a fixed rent; or a piece of land held by this tenure, the commonest in Scotland.

Feuar: The tenant of a feu.

Kirktoun: A small nucleated settlement developed around a parish church within a rural parish.

Mercat cross: A market cross; stone crosses set on tall uprights as reminders of fair dealing and honesty where markets were held, found in north-west Europe from the twelfth century.

Miltoun: A hamlet attached to or adjoining a mill.

Neighbourhood: A local community, featuring housing and a variety of destinations necessary for daily life, including shops, offices, parks and civic buildings.

Neighbourhood centre: Central point of a neighbourhood, typically featuring amenities for the neighbourhood at large, including shops, offices, parkland and civic buildings.

Pattern book: A document articulating and illustrating the detailed design plans for a new community.

Pend: An archway or a covered way of passage, which passes within a block.

Toft: Burgage plot; the plot of a house or buildings.

Tollboth: The main municipal building of a burgh. Originally, they functioned as the place where tolls and customs were collected. Gradually, their purpose expanded to provide a council meeting room, court house and prison.

Transect: A cross-section of the environment showing a range of different habitats. Chapelton's rural-to-urban transect divides the human environment into six transect zones, which describe the physical form and character of a place according to the density and intensity of its land use and urbanism.

Tron: A public steelyard or weighing-machine within a burgh, set up in or near the market-place for the weighing of merchandise, particularly locally produced goods.

Vennel: A narrow alley or lane between houses.

Wynd: A narrow street, lane or alley, which passes within a block to provide access to houses or shops. Traditionally, wynds frequently follow a somewhat sinuous or curving course.

NOTES

INTRODUCTION

01 R. Isaacs, 'The Urban Picturesque: An aesthetic experience of urban pedestrian places', *Journal of Urban Design*, v. 5, n. 2, 2000, 146.

02 R. A. Nisbet, *The Quest for Community*, New York: Oxford University Press, 1969; S. B. Sarason, *The Psychological Sense of Community: Prospects for a community psychology*, San Francisco: Jossey-Bass, 1974.

03 R. Florida, C. Mellander and K. Stolarick, 'Beautiful Places: The role of perceived aesthetic satisfaction in community satisfaction', Working Paper Series, Martin Prosperity Institute, University of Toronto, 2009.

04 K. Leyden, A. Goldberg and P. Michelbach, 'Understanding the Pursuit of Happiness', *Urban Affairs Review*, v. 47, n. 6, November 2011, 861-88.

CHAPTER ONE

01 T. Kath, 'The Trading Privileges of the Royal Burghs of Scotland', *The English Historical Review*, v. 28, no. 111, July 1913, 454-7; P. Dennison and G. Simpson, 'Scotland', in D. Palliser (ed.), *The Cambridge Urban History of Britain*, v. 1, Cambridge: Cambridge University Press, 2000, p. 720.

02 E. Ewan, *Town Life in Fourteenth-Century Scotland*, Edinburgh: Edinburgh University Press, 1990, p. 1; Dennison and Simpson, op. cit., p. 718.

03 I. Campbell and M. Stewart, 'The Evolution of the Medieval and Renaissance City', in B. Edwards and P. Jenkins (eds), *Edinburgh: The Making of a Capital City*, Edinburgh: Edinburgh University Press, 2005, pp. 21-2.

04 I. Adams, *The Making of Urban Scotland*, London: Croom Helm, 1978, p. 33.

05 R. Rodger, 'The Evolution of Scottish Town Planning', in G. Gordon and B. Dicks, *Scottish Urban History*, Aberdeen: Aberdeen University Press, 1983, p. 75.

06 M. Lynch (ed.), *The Oxford Companion to Scottish History*, Oxford: Oxford University Press, 2011, p. 616.

07 Rodger, op. cit., p. 73.

08 Lynch, op. cit., p. 616.

09 N. T. Phillipson and R. Mitchison, 'Introduction', in N. T. Phillipson and R. Mitchison (eds), *Scotland in the Age of Improvement*, Edinburgh: Edinburgh University Press, 1970, p. 1.

10 M. Glendinning and A. MacKechnie, *Scottish Architecture*, London: Thames and Hudson, 2004, p. 94.

11 B. Harris, *The Scottish Town in the Age of Enlightenment 1740-1820*, Edinburgh: Edinburgh University Press, 2014, p. 104.

12 M. Glendinning, R. MacInnes and A. MacKechnie, *A History of Scottish Architecture: From the Renaissance to the Present Day*, Edinburgh: Edinburgh University Press, 1996, p. 169.

13 C. McKean, 'The Incivility of Edinburgh New Town', in W. Brogden (ed.), *The Neo-Classical Town: Scottish Contributions to Urban Design since 1750*, Edinburgh: The Rutland Press, 1996, pp. 39-40.

14 D. Defoe, *A Tour Through the Whole Island of Great Britain*, New Haven: Yale University Press, 1991, p. 131.

15 A. J. Youngson, *The Making of Classical Edinburgh 1750-1840*, Edinburgh: Edinburgh University Press, 1966, pp. 3-12.

16 McKean, op. cit., pp. 39-40.

17 Youngson, op. cit., pp. 70-1.

18 McKean, op. cit., p. 41.

19 Ibid., p. 44.

20 For example, the Gayfield estate was built from 1807 on land owned by James Jolie; the Moray estate was begun in 1822 by the Earl of Moray; the Raeburn estate, owned by the painter Henry Raeburn, was constructed from 1813-30.

21 Glendinning et al, op. cit., p. 173.

22 Youngson, op. cit., pp. 81-2.

23 C.Whatley, 'John Galt and Scottish Social History in the Era of Enlightenment and Urbanisation', unpublished paper, University of Glasgow, 2014, p. 6.

24 W. H. Fraser and C. Lee (eds), *Aberdeen 1800-2000: A New History*, East Linton: Tuckwell, 2000, pp. 22-3.

25 D. Macaulay, 'The Growth of a New Town', in E. Dennison, D. Ditchburn and M. Lynch (eds), *Aberdeen Before 1800*, East Linton: Tuckwell Press, 2002, p. 416.

26 L. Philip, 'The Creation of Settlements in Rural Scotland: Planned villages in Dumfries and Galloway, 1730-1850', *Scottish Geographical Journal*, v. 119, no. 2, 78; Adams, op. cit., p. 57; R. Millman, *The Making of the Scottish Landscape*, London: B. T. Batsford, 1975, p. 175.

27 Millman, op. cit., p. 103.

28 T. C. Smout, 'The Landowner and the Planned Village in Scotland, 1730-1830', in Phillipson and Mitchison (eds), op. cit., p. 77.

29 Philip, op. cit., 77-9, 93; D. Lockhart, 'Scottish Village Plans: A preliminary analysis', *Scottish Geographical Magazine*, v. 96, 1980, 149; Adams, op. cit., p. 61.

30 Rodger, op. cit., p. 82; Adams, op. cit., p. 65; D. Lockhart, 'Migration to Planned Villages in Scotland between 1725 and 1850', *Scottish Geographical Magazine*, v. 102, 1986, 165.

31 Lockhart, 1986, op. cit., 169.

32 Smout, op. cit., p. 95.

33 Lockhart, 1980, op. cit., 150.

34 Ibid., 150.

35 P. Nuttgens, 'The Planned Villages of North-East Scotland', in Brogden, op. cit., pp. 28-9; Glendinning et al, op. cit., p. 181.

36 Almost nothing of Gillespie Graham's extravagant 1811 plan for Kyleakin was built. Glendinning and MacKechnie, op. cit., pp. 115-18.

37 Ibid., p. 114.

38 Landowners sometimes erected an inn, courthouse or church in the villages.

39 D. Maudlin, 'Regulating the Vernacular: The impact of building regulations in the eighteenth-century Highland planned village', *Vernacular Architecture*, v. 35, 2004, 41.

40 H. Woolmer, 'Grantown-on-Spey: An eighteenth-century new town', *The Town Planning Review*, v. 41, n. 3, July 1970, 241.

41 Lockhart, 1980, op. cit., 152.

42 D. Lockhart, 'The Planned Villages of Aberdeenshire: The evidence from newspapers', *Scottish Geographical Magazine*, v. 94, 1978, 96; Philip, op. cit., 80.

43 Adams, op. cit., p. 71.

44 These tended to be those villages founded by the Forfeited Estates Commissioners in the Highlands, which was then characterised by political tumult. Smout, op. cit., p. 93; Lockhart, 1980, op. cit., 155.

45 D. Turnock, *The Historical Geography of Scotland since 1707*, Cambridge: Cambridge University Press, 2005, p. 92.

46 Nuttgens, op. cit., p. 26.

47 A. Alexander, *Britain's New Towns: Garden cities to sustainable communities*, Abingdon: Routledge, 2009, p. 70.

48 The target population was raised to 70,000 by 1960.

49 Alexander, op. cit., p. 113; Adams, op. cit., p. 215.

50 M. Glendinning, 'Modernity, Urbanity and Rationalism: New Towns of the twentieth century', in Brogden, op. cit., p. 110.

51 Alexander, op. cit., p. 115.

52 Ibid., p. 121.

53 Ibid., p. 121.

54 Ibid., p. 82.

55 M. Hughes (ed.), *The Letters of Lewis Mumford and Frederic J. Osborn: A transatlantic dialogue, 1938-1970*, Bath: Adams and Dart, 1971, p. 229.

56 L. Downie Jr., 'The Disappointing New Towns of Great Britain', *Washington Post*, 1 November 1972.

57 Scottish Government Communities Analysis Division (Housing Statistics).

58 Scottish Council of Economic Advisers, 'First Annual Report of the Scottish Council of Economic Advisers', December 2008, p. 44. Online. www. scotland.gov. uk/topics/economy/councileconomic-advisers/annual-reports. [Accessed 8 December 2017.]

59 J. Callcutt, 'Callcutt Review of Housebuilding Delivery', London: Department for Communities and Local Government, 2007, p. 65.

60 G. MacLeod, 'New Urbanism/Smart Growth in the Scottish Highlands: Mobile policies and post-politics in local development planning', *Urban Studies*, 2013, 2; M. Hebbert, 'New Urbanism – the Movement in Context', *Built Environment*, v. 29, no. 3, 2003, 196-6.

61 H. Gillette, *Civitas by Design: Building better communities, from the Garden City to the New Urbanism*, Philadelphia: University of Pennsylvania Press, 2010, p. 117.

62 A. Marshall, 'A tale of two towns tells a lot about this thing called New Urbanism', *Built Environment*, v. 29, no. 3, 2003, 233.

63 There are numerous exceptions to this rule, notably Prospect in Colorado, USA.

64 R. Rogers, 'Speaking the Same Urban Language', *Building Design*, 13 August 2004, 10; A. Passell, *Building the New Urbanism*, Abingdon: Routledge, 2013, p. 96.

65 MacLeod, op. cit., 3.

CHAPTER TWO

01 Duke of Fife, discussion with authors, 13 September 2017.

02 Ibid.

03 Duchess of Fife, discussion with authors, 13 September 2017.

04 Duke of Fife, discussion.

05 Ibid.

06 The Aberdeenshire Local Development Plan was formally adopted by the Scottish Government in June 2012.

07 The overall site area of Chapelton will yield a total of approximately 8,000 houses, but, as this is almost double the housing allocation of the LDP, the settlement was planned to be developed in phases. Therefore, the outline planning application made provision for a standalone community of 4,045 dwellings, which could grow with the adoption of a new LDP in 2023.

08 G. Murray (town architect, Brooks Murray Architects), discussion with authors, 23 August 2017.

09 A. Aboyne (managing director, AJC Homes), discussion with authors, 30 January 2018.

10 Murray, discussion.

11 Duchess of Fife, discussion.

12 Duke of Fife, discussion.

13 Ibid.

14 Aboyne, discussion.

15 Duchess of Fife, discussion.

16 Ibid.

17 M. Knox and D. Alcock, 'Approaches to Community Governance: Models for mixed tenure communities', Bristol: Policy Press, 2002, p. 18.

18 A. Duany, email correspondence with authors, 1 May 2018.

19 J. Stephen (managing director, A & J Stephen), discussion with authors, 6 February 2018.

20 K. Slowe (former managing director, ZeroC), discussion with authors, 26 January 2018.

21 J. Benton (landscape architect, Benton Scott-Simmons), discussion with authors, 15 January 2018.

CHAPTER THREE

01 A. Duany, email correspondence with authors, 1 May 2018.

02 E. Talen, 'Help for Urban Planning: The transect strategy', *Journal of Urban Design*, v. 7, n. 3, 2002, 294.

03 A. Cuthbert, *Understanding Cities*, London: Routledge, 2011, p. 125; R. Mantho, *The Urban Section*, London: Routledge, 2015, p. 12.

04 P. Geddes, 'Report on the Towns in the Madras Presidency', Madura, 1912, p. 91. Quoted in J. Tyrwhitt (ed.), *Patrick Geddes in India*, London: Lund Humphries, 1947, p. 22.

05 A. Duany and E. Talen, 'Transect Planning', *Journal of the American Planning Association*, v. 68, n. 3, 2002, 255.

06 Ibid., 247.

07 J. Benton (landscape architect, Benton Scott-Simmons), in discussion with authors, 15 January 2018.

08 Duany, correspondence.

09 Duke of Fife, in discussion with authors, 13 September 2017.

10 Benton, discussion.

11 P. Smith, *The Dynamics of Delight: Architecture and Aesthetics*, London: Routledge, 2003, p. 212.

12 J. Ruskin, *The Seven Lamps of Architecture*, London: Waverley Book Co., 1849, p. 8.

13 N. Boys-Smith, 'The Homes London Needs: A Direct Planning Revolution for London', Policy Exchange, February 2016, p. 7.

14 E. West, 'Classical Architecture Makes us Happy', *The Spectator*, 15 March 2017. Online. https://blogs.spectator. co.uk/2017/03/new-tory-manifesto-make-beauty-affordable/. [Accessed 30 January 2018.]

15 E. Buitelaar and F. Schilder, 'The Economics of Style: Measuring the Price Effect of Neo-Traditional Architecture in Housing', *Real Estate Economics*, v. 45, 2017. Online. https://onlinelibrary.wiley. com/doi/pdf/10.1111/1540-6229.12137. [Accessed 30 January 2018.]

16 Benton, discussion.

17 Duany, correspondence.

18 Benton, discussion.

19 Ibid.

EPILOGUE

01 W. Ostrowski, 'Sir Ebenezer Howard in Poland', *Town and Country Planning*, v. 34, n. 11, November 1966, 511-12.

ACKNOWLEDGEMENTS

The authors are indebted to the help of many people in the preparation of this book. To all those who gave their time and assistance we extend our thanks. Special thanks go to The Duke and Duchess of Fife, Alistair Aboyne, Kim Slowe, John Stephen, Gavin Murray, Pablo Fernandez, Janet Benton, Andrés Duany, Chris Pattison and Stephanie Gray.

Acknowledgements also go to Alex Woolley and Paul Felton of Common Curiosity for designing the book, to photographer Neale Smith who was responsible for many of the photos of Chapelton that feature within its pages, to Felipe Fuentes of Brooks Murray Architects for producing the plans of Chapelton and to Shuyou Zhang for the historic town plans that illustrate Chapter One.

PICTURE CREDITS

INDEX